DEVE
TOU
DESTINATIONS

POLICIES AND PERSPECTIVES

Jonathan Bodlender
Alan Jefferson
Carson Jenkins
Leonard Lickorish

LONGMAN

Longman Group UK Ltd
Westgate House, The High,
Harlow, Essex CM20 1YR

Reprinted 1994

A catalogue record for this book is available from the British Library.

ISBN 0-582-07805-9

Printed in Great Britain by Antony Rowe Ltd,
Chippenham, Wiltshire

Contents

Foreword

The authors have each concentrated on one important area of the wide ranging subject of tourist development, in co-operation to present an overall review in four parts:

Part I	Market product relationships
Part II	Development strategies
Part III	Administrative structure for tourism development
Part IV	Planning in action

This commentary on the subject focuses attention on the destination, as well as the factors, forces and agents which influence and together determine the *product* and its production.

There are separate roles for the public and the private sectors, and a vast field where partnership action is involved. The two sectors are tightly linked: just as in marketing and production there is both a competitive and a co-operative function for all the interests if efficient operations are to result. The individual interests and traders are independent of each other in decisions and action but at the same time there is an interdependence notably in the context of a common destination which they serve.

Thus the exploration of the boundaries of public and private sector responsibility and of the co-operative and competitive areas and functions is essential if the destination is to set favourable conditions for development leading to a prosperous trade which will enrich the residents economically and socially, and satisfy their visitors.

Tourism can claim to be Europe's largest single trade. Forecasts of future growth suggest massive potential for the future. But there are major changing trends; a more volatile clientele; and problems as well as opportunities in exploiting the potential. Greater interest in and concern about non-economic costs and benefits will need to be given more attention, especially regarding the environment, for example protecting landscape, the countryside generally and the cultural heritage of treasures, not least historic towns and buildings. Tourism can conserve as well as disturb. Thus the management of tourist resources, which includes the development of the product and its marketing is increasingly a key aspect of the industry's co-operation in the role played by the public sector.

There is a serious weakness in the machinery of government dealing with tourism in its co-ordination, and co-operation with operators whether state or privately owned. Government policies or lack of them suggest an obsolescence in public administration devoted to tourism. The issues of yesterday get as much attention as present needs. Political will is often lacking. The necessary cooperative organisation representing all key tourism interest because of poor liaison may be weak and ineffective. There is a common responsibility in making good these deficiencies. Destinations through the local authority can press Central Government to clarify tourism policy and improve machinery for liaison. The operating sectors likewise can establish working relationships with each other and with the destination controllers. While there may be good vertical trade organisation (national associations for hotels, resorts, buses etc) horizontal co-ordination is lacking.

These are matters of prime concern because there is enough evidence to show that market forces alone cannot be relied upon to ensure satisfactory and continuing growth. The ebb and flow of traffic responding to market forces alone without the guiding hand of the destination manager will not provide optimum economic and social benefit. There must be a positive attempt to guide the destination's future through carefully planned and co-ordinated marketing and the right conditions for investment and operation. This is a complex and co-operative task, but with great rewards if professionally executed.

Part I: Market product relationships

Alan Jefferson

1 Travel, tourism and its potential benefits

Tourism is arguably even now the world's largest industry. As a consequence the practise of tourism is becoming increasingly sophisticated: marketers today must concern themselves with a skilful balance between quantity and quality while developers and providers of tourist products must concern themselves with conservation as well as the quality of the experience. The environment is a delicate resource which must be nurtured. Markets are dynamic, becoming more specialised and more competitive.

Tourism development is concerned with a wide range of services – transport, accommodation, attractions, the infrastructure. Products can be developed for tourists and used by local people and the converse is also true. The private sector is concerned with profit while the public sector is concerned with national benefits presented through politics which can embrace economic factors (balance of payments, employment), social issues, environmental factors, political–economic (Japanese 'exports' of international travellers) or national pride (the recent Australian and French bicentennials, Expos, Olympic Games).

Tourism is a complex trade covering all movements of people outside their own community for all purposes except migration or regular daily work. It is not a single industry but a movement of people, a demand force. It is a major economic activity which is highly competitive: a major employer, and a global phenomenon. It has its up side of tangible benefits: economic – wealth creation, foreign exchange earner; creator of employment; conserver of traditions, crafts and the heritage. It also has its downside inasmuch as it can bring with it erosion and sometimes even destruction of the environment; local people can be exploited; cultures sacrificed. Unbridled development can however be avoided with good and careful management of the resource. The long term view can prevail over the quick return. Government either directly or through its agencies may intervene to manage the tourism resource. This can take the form of incentives or controls.

Definition of tourism and the tourist

In 1968 the Statistical Commission of the United Nations approved the following:

> For statistical purposes the term 'visitor' describes any person visiting a country other than that in which he has his normal place of residence for any reason other than following an occupation remunerated from within the country visited.[1]

The International Union of Official Tourist Organisations (IUOTO) later to become the World Tourist Organisation (WTO) supported this description but subdivided the term visitor:

> Tourist, ie temporary visitor staying at least twenty – four hours in the country visited, the purpose of whose journey can be classified under one of the following headings:
>
> 1. Leisure (recreation, holiday, health, study, religion and sport)
> 2. Business, family, mission, meeting.
>
> Excursionist, ie temporary visitor staying less than twenty – four hours in the country visited (including travellers on cruises). The statistics should not include travellers, who in the legal sense do not enter a country (air travellers who do not leave an airports' transit area and similar cases).[2]

All too often the term tourist is taken to mean the foreign holidaymaker and has become a pejorative label, when in fact a tourist is someone who may be travelling for many other reasons apart from pleasure and may well be a native of the country or even local to the area. Certainly the developer of a tourism product almost certainly needs to look beyond a strict interpretation of the definition of tourist and include the day visitor in demand projections. In practice, tourism and travel merges with day trips for planner, developer and visitor alike.

While the WTO definitions were developed to cover international travel they can equally well be used to define domestic travel. Indeed traveller, in many ways, is a much better word than tourist though travel industry may be too restrictive to describe tourism. Travel represents the economic incidence of the mobile population. Gilbert claims:

> The use of the term tourism has led to a range of complex meanings which have become associated with: the movement of people; a sector of the economy; an identifiable industry; services which need to be provided for travellers. The problem we face with tourism is that in defining its industry we attempt to isolate a particular type of consumer (ie the tourist as opposed to the local shopper, local traveller etc) and

> we do not focus on the wider aspects of the provider or producer of the service.[3]

Since the definition of tourist adopted by WTO is not simply restricted to those who travel for leisure or pleasure it follows that tourism is not restricted to transport, accommodation, catering and leisure facilities but also embraces conference centres, exhibition halls, hospitals and medical treatment centres, schools and colleges, religious retreats and many others. Gilbert argues that:

> The tourist industry is treated as a composite whole, yet it is an amalgam of different service industries providing satisfaction for a wide range of needs. Tourism as a generic term provides a simplistic focal point of activity which may not characterise the overall functions of its definition.[4]

As a service trade tourism is capital intensive to a major degree in infrastructure and plant.

Tourism embraces a very wide range of products and the tourism market is not a homogeneous one but made up of many segments and sub-segments. It is necessary to understand the motivations and the characteristics of individual segments not simply to identify meaningful groups at which to target the marketing effort but also to identify product needs.

The tourist product

It is essential that the development of the tourism product must be marketing orientated. 'The quality of the experience is the product itself'.[5] Tourism is a fragmented industry involving many interests in the provision of the satisfying experience.

> There is much confusion over the definition of the product. Tourism is not a sunny beach, a grand hotel, a flight or indeed any particular attraction. It is a satisfying activity at a desired destination. The two features must be present together. From this it can be seen that the complexities of tourism are substantial because a wide range of options, services and suppliers are involved. Furthermore, although in creating any one tourism product many interests are involved which are interdependent, they are also independent of each other and often in competition.[6]

So product development must be concerned with the provision or enhancement of services, transport, accommodation, attractions and infrastructure and designed to enhance the experience of the visitor. The tourism product is a collection of physical and service features together with symbolic associations which are expected to fulfil the needs of the buyer.

Statistics

Also see appendix at end of chapter.

An understanding of statistics, their availability and limitations and skill in their analysis and interpretation is a prerequisite of effective marketing and key to successful product development. The basic unit of measurement is the *visit* and while it is desirable that this unit should comply with the WTO definitions it is not always so. A country's official statistics may well not conform to the internationally accepted definitions. In one country international visits may be determined from immigration controls (landing cards). In another they may be computed from hotel registrations, while in a third they may be based on bank transactions and currency exchanged. Each method has its limitations and it is even more difficult to measure the visitor expenditure. The best, though expensive, method of measuring visits, spend and a series of other data such as seasonality, regional spread, purpose of visit, country of residence etc is the sample survey.

Whatever the problems and limitations, official statistics can be put to practical use. Very often there are alternative sources which can be used to crosscheck the official sources. For example the passengers carried by ferry companies and airlines from Scandinavia to Britain can be used as a check on the figures provided by the International Passenger Survey carried out as a sample survey by Government statisticians; the US Department of Commerce reports on spending by residents of the US in foreign countries; the German Holiday Travel Analysis (Reiseanalyse) provides very sophisticated data on an annual basis. The US Travel Data Center is an affiliate of the Travel Industry Association of America and is the national non-profit centre for travel and tourism research. Increasingly the Center is engaging in forecasting and interpreting trends affecting travel internationally.

Statistical data is needed on country for place of residence, country or region visited, purpose of visit, length of stay, basic socio–economic information (age, sex, occupation) and spend. The World Tourist Organisation (WTO) regularly publishes *World Travel and Tourism Statistics;* the Organisation for Economic Co–operation and Development (OECD), the Commission of the European Communities (EC), as well as National Tourist Offices publish statistical series. Interpretation of the figures such as the

British Tourist Authority's *Tourism Intelligence Quarterly* are also frequently issued. Some independent consultants summarise international data in a very helpful way and increasingly there is a trend to integrate consultancy services to provide data on several countries or across a number of disciplines on a consortium basis. The Economist Intelligence Unit publishes monthly *Travel and Tourism Analyst*[7] an invaluable source of business information and forecasts for all sectors of the industry.

Market research can be undertaken specifically to uncover data on a particular market or segment, attitudes, image or perception of a destination or product. Some National Tourist Offices carry out regular surveys of visitor satisfaction such as the British Tourist Authority's *Overseas Visitor Survey*.

Potential benefits of developing tourism for a destination

The critics of tourism argue that third world countries especially do not benefit from international travel, which encourages prostitution, drug trafficking, and causes damage to the environment and inflation. Furthermore, the tourism *earnings* flow out of the destination to shareholders elsewhere.

This charge, that tourism corrupts and destroys environments and cultures, may indeed be levelled at some developments. Undeniably the Spanish built too many hotels in Benidorm and on the Costa Brava and destroyed the beautiful beaches which had drawn the visitors in the first place. Turkey more recently has been in danger of repeating the mistake. There are cases too of cultures being overwhelmed by tourism. Certainly there is a price to pay. It may be environmental or cultural, social or economic. Yet it does not have to occur. Tourism can raise educational standards; bring renewed pride in cultures and crafts; conserve the heritage and historic buildings. Tourism's economic benefits can conserve the wildlife of a region. The arts and crafts of the Eskimo and the American Indian, the Mexican Indians and the Balinese have been reinvigorated by tourism. The Singaporean government is encouraging artists and craftsmen to form *living heritage groups* to sustain skills which would otherwise be in danger of dying out.

The facilities and attractions aimed at tourists are also available to local people. Many shops, pubs and restaurants could not survive without tourists, many historic houses and castles are sustained by tourism. On the other hand some world famous buildings in cities such as Athens and Venice are endangered by tourism. Towns and cities have been built to take the pressure of people but intensive pressure can bring severe wear and tear on the infrastructure. It is even more true of the countryside and the coastline, where paths designed for intermittent use can be eroded and littered. Tourism can threaten the ecology of the area. Yet it can involve local communities and bring benefits to the countryside.

Local community involvement is typified in mid Wales with their vital participation in the Mid Wales Festival of the Countryside which aims to maintain their unique heritage of countryside and culture. Elsewhere, self catering holiday cottages are being developed from redundant farm buildings. For example, a traditional oasthouse near Ashford, Kent has been converted into a self catering property which would otherwise have become derelict and demolished. The country house hotel is an uniquely British product and development of this product has saved a great number of houses which might otherwise have disappeared. Many barns have fallen into disuse and have emerged as budget accommodation for walkers and cyclists, providing simple bunkhouse self-catering facilities. The Federation National de Gites Ruraux de France, established in 1965 under the joint patronage of the Secretary of State for Tourism and the Minister of Agriculture, is perhaps the best known example of a marketing co-operative which has very successfully revitalised country cottages and other buildings which might otherwise have fallen into disrepair or even disappeared. Rural revitalisation can, properly managed, stem from tourism.

Views on tourism tend to be polarised. Is it an economic force for good; a sustainer of cultures and heritage; or is it a destroyer and a pollutant? It behoves us to examine the downside of tourism in order that evasive action can be taken and ideally built into the development at the planning stage. The benefits of tourism will only accrue to a destination if the right sort of development is planned for it. The industry is very fragmented and consists of many small operators who are individually concerned to develop a profitable enterprise.

Role of government

There is clearly an important role for governments in the development of the product as well as the marketing of the destination. It is essential for towns and regions as well as countries to have an effective tourism department. Tim O'Driscoll, writing on the role of government in tourism, says:

> In formulating a tourism policy, the government will have a number of possible options before it. It will have to decide, for example, the

> appropriate rate of growth which is planned in the tourism sector, whether to encourage mass tourism or to cultivate a slower and more selective growth. It will have to determine what should be the respective roles of the public and the private sector in developing the tourist industry and similarly of domestic and foreign capital. It must establish the due importance to be given to the needs of the tourism sector in plans for national and regional development and in so doing must take a decision regarding the timescale that it considers reasonable for planning forward investments in the tourism industry.
>
> In practice only governments can determine what is in the national interest. Ideally tourism should have little effect on the virtues of a destination and its inhabitants. Countries should simply be themselves *accepted and accepting*. But facilities for visitors must be provided and providing them can show how delicate a task it is to change standards without altering the essential character one wishes to retain. But national characteristics and natural amenities are the raw materials of tourism.[8]

Tourism is invariably dependent on government help in the provision of infrastructure – airports, roads, utilities, sewerage and services. With large-scale developments such as the Languedoc – Roussillon project there needs to be a formal structuring of responsibilities. This vast project on the Mediterranean between the Rhone delta and the Spanish border was such that no one organisation had the resources or ability to carry it out. At the same time a critical path had to be co-ordinated and planned. The roles of the State, the regional authorities and the private sector were clearly defined from the outset. Responsibility for the overall development plan was the State's as was acquisition of land and infrastructural development. The regional authorities participated in the development through the creation of four mixed economy companies. These companies having installed essential services sold the land at a price to recover costs to the private sector. Only then did the private sector move in to build the hotels and the apartment blocks, the shops and the villas, attractions and facilities.

Governments have a key role in providing incentives. In Britain, under the *Development of Tourism Act 1969*, provision was made for the Hotel Development Incentive Scheme, which provided grant aid for all new hotel rooms built during a three year period which provided en suite bathroom facilities. The intention was to stimulate a swift increase in internationally acceptable hotel accommodation so as to take full advantage of the tourism opportunities arising from the rapid growth in travel potentials and in air transport with the advent of the wide bodied jet. Governments can also influence tourism flows through legislation or controls, eg visas; civil aviation control – Greece refuses to accept outbound charters; control on hotel development – Malta will only permit the development of four star hotels currently.

Government's role is essential in these areas because of the national benefits which tourism brings as a wealth creator, job creator, earner of foreign currency. Tourism can bring about inner city regeneration; stem the flow of people from the countryside; sustain heritage and culture, arts and crafts; protect the environment and the wildlife of a region. Tourism improves international understanding among peoples. But the key to successful tourism development is in careful and controlled planning at both national and local levels as part of a total economic plan. Kendell claims that:

> Historically, tourism plans in one guise or another have been prepared for part or all of almost every country throughout the world – both developed and less developed – and, in some instances, on more than one occasion! Too often, however, such plans have either failed to be implemented or have been implemented and failed. The reasons underlying this tragic state of affairs are many and result, partly by accident or unforeseen circumstances – for example the oil crisis, Chernobyl, or acts of terrorism, but more often through culpable negligence on the part of the planner.
>
> Whilst the reasons for failure of tourism planning are many, there are four which are by far the most important.
>
> 1. A weak organisation structure which fails to establish the roles that should be played by the public and private sectors in implementing the plan, particularly in developing, marketing and monitoring the sector. In other words, the organisation fails to identify who does what, when and how.
> 2. A public sector that lacks the essential experience of the functions of a Tourism Development Corporation or those of a National Tourist Office (NTO).
> 3. Inadequate financial support for the NTO, leading to weak marketing and promotional activities.
> 4. A lack of experience and understanding of the tourism sector by the bi-lateral and multi-lateral aid agencies, resulting in poorly researched and inadequate or inappropriate projects.[9]

All too often a plan is developed without the market having been adequately researched to establish whether demand is viable. All too often investment is made in the product with inadequate thought to managing or marketing it.

The roles of governments are considered in greater depth in Part 3 Chapter 1.

References

1 Lickorish LJ *Reviews of United Kingdom Statistical Sources* Vol IV. Leisure and Tourism, Heinemann Educational Books, p 28
2 Lickorish LJ ibid p 27
3 Gilbert DC Conceptual issues in the meaning of tourism *Progress in Tourism Recreation and Hospitality Management*, Vol 2, 1990 Belhaven Press p 5
4 Gilbert DC ibid p 15
5 Parker Sir Peter *British Tourism – The Next 50 Years* 1979 BTA
6 Jefferson A, Lickorish LJ *Marketing tourism – A Practical Guide* 1989 Longman p 4
7 *Travel and Tourism Analyst* Economist Publications Ltd
8 O'Driscoll T *The Role of Government in Tourism. Tourism A Portrait* Horwath and Horwath (UK) Ltd November 1988. pp 47– 48
9 Kendell P *Planning The Tourism Product* ibid pp 44–45

Appendix

Extract from *Marketing Tourism – A Practical Guide* 1989. Longman

Statistics

Statistics of tourism are often criticised. They may not be comprehensive. Analysis may be limited particularly in regard to seasonal information. There are often bureaucratic delays and errors in description so that interpretation and use are difficult. Furthermore, system errors and statistical errors are quite common. Nevertheless statistics, however limited, are necessary, and useful if the figures are correctly described. There are ways of supplementing official data from trade information and through periodic sampling. Full knowledge of what figures are available, how to use them and how to be numerate, is an essential part of the marketing art.

The principal definitions of tourism have already been described. These are the bases for effective statistical systems. The key element in the generally accepted definition is the temporary stay, normally more than twenty-four hours and less than one year (after which the visitor is assumed to be a resident), and no income eamed at the destination visited. In other words, the visitor spend represents an injection of external 'income'.

Definitions also take account of day visits. These are important in domestic tourism but difficult to define and measure. In some countries (eg the USA) distances of one hundred miles have been taken as the dividing line between local and 'tourist' journeys. This may be arbitrary; the economic distinction is again a visit outside the area of residence involving spending of money not earned in the place visited. Commuters are clearly not tourists, even if they commute one hundred miles, as some do.

Official records may not conform to the agreed 'official' definitions, because the governmental systems of measurement are usually based on police controls at frontiers (immigration), or through hotel registration. The latter is common practice in many European countries where massive cross border flows make a full count impractical. Clearly hotel checks are unsatisfactory in many ways because they may not cover visits to camping sites, self-catering establishments, staying with friends and relatives etc. In other words fifty per cent or more of the traffic may not be measured. There are even more problems with value measurements to report tourist expenditure. The most effective method is through sample surveys, either at the frontier, at the destinations or through household surveys. Such surveys are difficult and expensive. So many countries resort to broad estimates based on bank records of foreign currency exchanged. The results are often substantially inaccurate.

In spite of many technical problems official figures can be helpful. Sometimes cross checks are possible, for example the US government Department of Commerce and other agencies report American visitor spending in European countries which can be compared with the figures produced by European governments. Provided definitions used, and limitations are carefully and exactly reported, the regular series of international and national travel statistics can be put to practical marketing use.

Categories of tourist statistics

There are four basic categories of measurement:

1. Traffic movement (volume) and visitor expenditure (representing economic value).
2. Information on the stock (capacity) and development of services and facilities for travellers.
3. Market research and intelligence, analysing demand and demand trends.
4. Checks and tests of effectiveness in operations. This would cover accupancy rates, load factors but also sales and marketing activity.

Statistical information needed

Commonly the basic unit of measurement is the 'visit', although some countries and some trades use the 'visitor night' ie one night stay by one person, as the standard. If the number of visitors is known then tourist nights are reported by length of stay checks. In practice many figures are reported as 'visitors' when the measure is in fact one person making one visit. A considerable number of travellers make a number of journeys. Some business men, for example, almost 'commute' across the Atlantic. Official records for foreign visitors to Britain are in fact separate visits and not people. For certain types of movement this distinction could be important in promotion and sales plans. The official records clearly aim to report visits to the destination concerned (the country, region, city or resort). Information is needed on:

1. the place of permanent residence of the visitor;
2. country, region or town (resort) visited;
3. purpose of visit (business, pleasure, health, education etc), the more detailed the classification the better, as this assists in valuable segmentation exercises;
4. length of stay in country, region or town (resort);

5. basic socio-economic information (age, sex, status, nationality, occupation). There is a limit to the detail, but for market research purposes education, income and indications of behaviour or 'life style' groups can be very useful.

There is inevitably a conflict between the desire to facilitate travel, especially across frontiers, and to remove tiresome official checks and the desire to collect data. If basic volume and value checks are carried out much of the detail can be collected through sampling. This can be very expensive in tourism, and is often best done as explained later through cooperative action with the trades concerned.

Statistical methods

Principal methods can be summarised as follows:

1. Household sample surveys, at the visitors' place of residence (before, but more usually, after the journey).
2. International frontier or port surveys, counting or sampling visitors on arrival or departure. This is the principal means of collecting Britain's official international travel records.
3. Traffic counts, sampling travellers en route, at termini or at traffic cordons.
4. Surveys in the destination (resort) areas during their stay.
5. Accommodation records and sampling at visitors' place of stay (hotels etc).
6. Trade information. This can take many forms, most commonly sales analysis. It also includes informative data from in flight surveys on airlines, hotel occupancy data, and although not much used, travel agent and tour operator information.

Some of the trades, notably the airlines, produce very detailed and helpful traffic information eg International Air Transport Association (IATA) and Association of European Airlines. National associations and some independent consultants summarise international data regularly in a very helpful way. International bodies are in a position to carry out useful and practical studies. The World Tourist Organisation (WTO) regularly publishes a statistical digest of the official travel statistics of all the major countries. The Organisation for Economic Co-operation and Development (OECD) publishes annually an economic and statistical report on all aspects of tourism by the principal industrialised countries in the world which account for some eighty per cent of all world travel. This is one of the best sources of vital trend information in world travel. Recently the Commission of the European Communities (EC) carried out some research into tourism, and this may become a source of new and helpful records.

2 Tourism – past and present

For the first time in 1984 international tourist arrivals went through the 300 million barrier. Only a decade before it was about 200 million. The present level is about 400 million. Yet, probably no more than ten per cent of total tourist movements throughout the world are international. No data is available on a global basis, but this would appear to be a fair estimate based on data which is available in some countries. Day trippers add substantially to this figure. American Express studies estimate total world travel spend – domestic and foreign – as three trillion US dollars.

Tourism is big business

The principle, conceived and articulated at the first United Nations' Conference on Tourism in 1963, that 'Tourism is a basic and most desirable human activity, deserving the praise and encouragement of all peoples and all governments' seems to have been embraced mightily. International tourist arrivals have increased from 81 million in 1962 to 404 million in 1989. For many countries tourism is the single most important activity in its economy.

Sixty years ago the majority of people, even in developed countries, took short trips – the Londoner to Margate or Southend, the Glaswegian 'doon the water' to one of the Clyde resorts. When travel became easier horizons became extended and jorneys were further afield. Jumbo jets in the 70s made international travel easier and indeed cheaper. Transatlantic fares are less than half the real price of twenty-five years ago when real incomes were much lower.

Sir Peter Parker, giving the Golden Jubilee Lecture on the Come to Britain movement in 1979, said:

> The growth decade had started, 1970 was a turning point for coming to Britain ..... improved mobility which was above all symbolised by the advent of the wide bodied jet. Three to four times the number of

> people started to arrive without any increase in the number of aircraft movements. It took forty years to reach the five million total of 1969 overseas visitors. It took ten years to more than double that figure to reach the twelve million welcome invaders estimated for 1979.[1]

In 1990 the figure achieved was about eighteen million.

Tourism growth has come from the developed world where disposable incomes and leisure time have increased with affluence. Some ninety per cent of world travel is accounted for by the residents of OECD member states. Travel has become an expectation of the masses in the industrialised world and we are beginning to see this extending to many undeveloped countries.

With affluence came increased car ownership, which in turn made the population more mobile. In the United Kingdom car ownership increased from 5.5 million in 1960 to around 23 milion in 1990. In Europe today the car is the most frequently used method of transport for holidaymakers. Car ownership continues to increase year by year. The total cars registered in Europe reached approximately 150 million by 1985. In that year the EC survey *Europeans and their Holidays* recorded over 70 per cent of all holidays as taken in private cars, and even holidays in European countries outside country of residence depended on private cars for transport in over 50 per cent of the total. Increased ownership of television and more recently video has again widened horizons and given people a taste for travel, a wish to see new countries and peoples.

This massive increase in travel has been accompanied by substantial investment in the tourism plant in receiving countries. In the 1960s there was an explosive growth in Mediterranean and Adriatic resorts, alas at the expense of the Northern Europeans' cold water resorts. England has gained more than 400 new attractions over the past five years and some, like the Jorvik Centre in York, the Guiness World of Records and Tower Bridge in London, Wigan Pier and Blackpool's Sandcastle in North West England, are already topping half a million visits each year. Florida and Queensland have seen massive developments in infrastructure, accommodation and attractions. Singapore's hotel stock has burgeoned. Mexico has several new resorts as has Thailand and Turkey. More and more developers are moving into the tourism and leisure sector.

Fashion plays an important part in travel and changes in lifestyle have affected the choice of destination and the requirements at the destination. People in developed countries are marrying and having families later. They are living together and these dual income households have the will and the wherewithal to travel.

People are retiring earlier and living longer. They have the ability and the desire to travel and they are growing as a proportion of the total population. At the same time social legislation, especially in Europe, has increased the leisure time available; longer holidays and five-day weeks have become the norm. As developed countries moved out of their industrial, manufacturing periods into a post-industrial service era there was no longer a need to close down the factory or the workplace. Holidays could be staggered; short breaks became possible. The traditional patterns of holiday taking were changing.

In Britain some resorts lost their way and the will to develop. Some, like Brighton and Bournemouth, changed direction and, having segmented their markets, went additionally for conference business and English language students. Thousands of small hotels and boarding houses became retirement homes. The boom in cheap holidays at Mediterranean resorts threatened the future of British seaside resorts but they are increasingly adapting to the new demands for shorter holidays, for off-peak holidays. Blackpool now claims to offer more nightlife than anywhere in the country outside London. Brighton has invested in a marina, a conference centre, and a number of new hotels. Bournemouth has a new conference centre as does Torbay. They seem ready for a renaissance.

Some of Britain's larger industrial cities, Glasgow, Manchester, Liverpool, and Birmingham for example, have forged ahead in developing a significant tourism industry responding to the changing patterns of demand. They mirror the developments in other cities such as Baltimore and Toronto. We have seen a shopping revolution and tourism playing an increasingly important role in the shopping and leisure equation. Shopping remains the biggest single sector of overseas visitor spend in Britain.

The high spenders are however the business travellers. In Britain they account for about a quarter of all international visits and embrace visits to trade fairs and exhibitions, conference delegates, study visits, incentive travel as well as independent business travel. The latter can sometimes be extended into a leisure trip and sometimes the business traveller can be persuaded to bring his or her spouse. According to Horwath and Horwath, business travellers account for over 55 per cent of worldwide demand for accommodation in four and five star hotels. In the USA business travellers account for almost 50 per cent of all airline trips. Business travel is growing faster than total travel.

There has also been a significant increase in special interest travel based on hobbies or activities. These span the age spectrum: senior citizens are as likely to take a walking holiday as the young traveller. The new lifestyles and behaviour patterns were beginning to manifest themselves in holidays. Activity holidays, cultural pursuits, packages based on theatre, have developed fast where value for money rather than cheapness is the important factor.

> The Grand Tour of Europe was an accepted part of education for people of *quality* in 18th century Britain and Ireland. Indeed the history of mass tourism in Britain which did much to shape the early patterns of Europe's tourism industry, emphasised the educational and cultural values much more than the commercial gain.
>
> Today's mass movement has resulted in commercial dominance and the eclipse of many voluntary bodies. Paradoxically, with the mega mass movements and the introduction of the words tourist and tourism in the English language at least the respect and the understanding of social and human qualities have diminished with perhaps an over concentration on the economic values alone.[2]

Perhaps with the growth of special interest travel we are seeing a return to the social and human values of tourism, the educational and cultural values, where price is secondary to the buyer and commercial gain is a reasonable expectation of the provider. Lifestyles change relatively quickly, even within the same generation. There is a powerful fashion in lifestyles rooted in the revolution in information technologies. This together with changes in demographics, leisure time, and wealth are providing a large potential market for specialist activity in sports, hobbies, education, and culture. Much of this finds expression in travel, pursuing leisure activity away from the home environment, where the change of scene adds lustre to well practised pastimes.

Incentive travel has burgeoned. Companies use great expectations to motivate great achievers and the prize is exceptional quality in the form of travel and experience at the destination. The incentive trip is special, unique, memorable and increasingly seen as the highest form of award for achievement. This segment was recently surveyed by the European Travel Commission (ETC) and the report suggested that incentive travel is growing fastest of all with an estimated five million trips a year currently.

Educational travel has become substantial – English language study for people of all ages as English increasingly becomes the international language of communication. English is the official or joint official language in more than 70 countries and states around the world, after which comes French in 34, Arabic in 22 and Spanish in 19. Britain attracts well over half a million visitors who come specifically to study English. Management courses, conferences and seminars are huge generators of visitor traffic.

Senior citizens have emerged as a powerful movement in both domestic and international travel.

There has been a significant increase in independent travel, away from the inclusive package in some countries, especially Northern Europe. There has been a larger number of holidays taken as leisure time and disposable incomes grows.

These new streams of traffic have been turned to advantage by the marketers who have helped turn a seasonal cottage industry catering largely for a domestic market into an international industry as substantial as any in the world. Figure 2.1 shows how the United Kingdom has performed in addressing the seasonality challenge over the ten years 1979 – 1989.

Figure 2.1 Visitors to UK by month 1980–1989

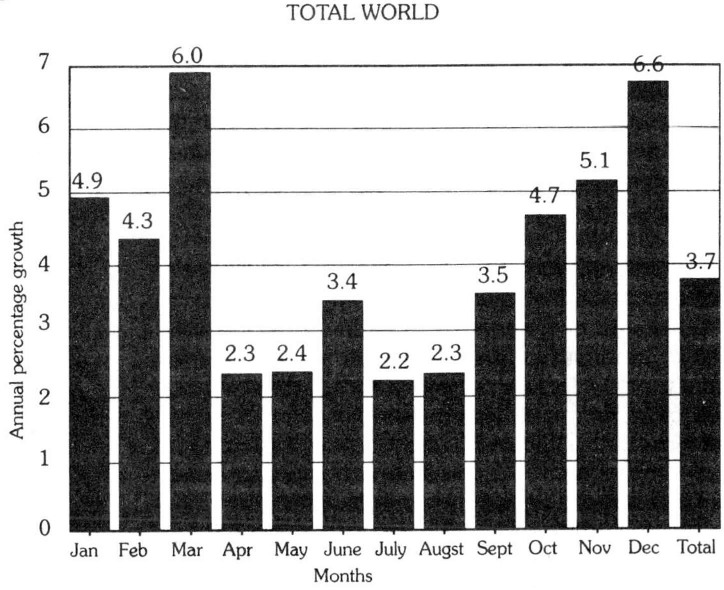

Source: *International Passenger Survey*

All months except April, May, June, July, August and September have recorded annual increases of more than the average for overseas visitor arrivals. Upgraded accommodation and all-weather facilities have allowed the big operators to extend the season, filling gaps whenever and wherever they occur. In 1982 the European Travel Commission (ETC) and the European Tourism Action Group (ETAG) organised with the operators a three year experimental effort in Malta, Cyprus and Rhodes to promote the shoulder months. Cyprus recorded a 39 per cent increase over the three years.

Table 2.1 International travel: arrivals and receipts 1950 to 1988

	International Tourist Arrivals			International Tourist Receipts		
Year	Numbers (000)	% change	Index (1950=100)	US.$ millions	% change	Index (1950=100)
1950	25,300	n.a	100	2,100	n.a	100
1960	69,300	+10	274	6,900	+19	327
1961	75,300	+9	298	7,300	+6	347
1962	81,300	+8	322	8,000	+10	382
1963	90,000	+11	356	8,900	+11	423
1964	104,500	+16	413	10,100	+13	480
1965	112,700	+8	446	11,600	+15	553
1966	119,800	+6	474	13,300	+15	635
1967	129,500	+8	512	14,500	+8	688
1968	130,900	+1	518	15,000	+4	714
1969	143,100	+9	566	16,800	+12	800
1970	159,700	+12	632	17,900	+7	852
1971	172,200	+8	681	20,900	+16	993
1972	181,900	+6	719	24,600	+18	1,172
1973	190,600	+5	754	31,100	+26	1,479
1974	197,100	+3	780	33,800	+9	1,611
1975	214,400	+9	848	40,700	+20	1,938
1976	220,700	+3	873	44,400	+9	2,116
1977	239,100	+8	946	55,600	+25	2,649
1978	257,400	+8	1,018	68,800	+24	3,278
1979	274,000	+6	1,084	83,300	+21	3,968
1980	284,800	+4	1,127	102,400	+23	4,874
1981	288,800	+1	1,143	104,300	+2	4,966
1982	286,800*	−1	1,134	98,600*	−5	4,696
1983	284,400*	−1	1,125	98,500*	0	4,689
1984	311,200*	+9	1,231	102,500*	+4	4,882
1985	325,700*	+5	1,288	108,100*	+5	5,147
1986	332,900*	+2	1,317	130,100*	+20	6,196
1987	358,700	+8	1,419	158,700	+22	7,558
1988	390,000P	+9	1,541	195,000P	+23	9,285

Note: Arrivals are rounded to nearest 100,000 and receipts to nearest US $100m
* Revised estimates
n.a. not available
P preliminary estimates
Source: World Tourism Organization.

Perhaps the single most important trend to emerge in recent years, which will undoubtedly continue to gather momentum, is the move away from volume in the quest for quality tourism. The British Government has recently moved towards a policy of quality tourism; Malta will now only allow hotel development if they are four or five star; Spain and Portugal have to some extent changed their marketing thrust in favour of quality tourism. Thailand, which attracts about six million visitors a year, is moving out of the numbers game and aiming, with increased funding for the Tourism Authority of Thailand (TAT), to trade up and improve the quality of holidays spent there. Overdevelopment of resorts will be curbed, marketing is no longer price led but selective and quality led. The operators are beginning to listen to the market and the days of the cheap package to the Mediterranean beaches is becoming a thing of the past. Travellers are becoming more sophisticated, adventurous and, above all, discerning.

The last thirty years can be seen from a distance as falling into two parts (see Table 2.1). The beginnings of the mass travel movement in the 1960s accelerating with the advent of wide bodied jets in 1970 and the substantial growth only being halted in 1973 with major recession. Until then the market had developed in a fairly unsophisticated way and was highly seasonal. Then came a second set back in 1981 but tourism remained remarkably resilient and expansion followed the pause. It was in the early 1980s that new markets and new segments emerged, when seasonality was first challenged, quality and value for money were increasingly demanded. Specialist appeals growing in a widening range of leisure activity, coupled with rising prosperity and wealth in the industrialised countries benefiting from the revolution in technologies, and a great expansion in leisure time were the factors leading to the creation of a number of mini-mass markets, varying greatly in characteristics and behaviour. Change will accelerate. Marketers will need to identify change: producers and developers will need to respond to it. Standards have improved; competition has intensified; and the expectations of the traveller are much higher. One thing is certain though, by the 1980s the economic and social significance of tourism was established.

References

1 Parker, Sir Peter *British Tourism – The Next 50 Years* Golden Jubilee lecture. British Tourist Authority. 26 November 1979. p 9

2 Lickorish, LJ *The European Experience.* Speech to the Fifth International Conference. Peace Through Tourism – Shadow or Substance? 25 – 27 April 1990

3 Trends in tourism

Tourism and leisure are here to stay but if they are to progress they will need to adapt to demographic trends, to changes in fashion, changes in climate, changes in attitude. Destinations are being scrutinised by an increasingly sophisticated clientele – the international traveller – and by the conservationists. The appreciation of countryside and wilderness, concern for conservation and the environment, will become much more important over the next decade.

Those who are aware of the changes afoot will waste no effort on fighting them but rather will look for marketing opportunities within them. Increasingly though developers of tourism product will need to apply the following criteria:

1. Is there a market?
2. Is it viable economically?
3. Is it socially compatible?
4. Is it environmentally acceptable?

Is there a market?

The evolution of demand for international tourism on the global scale has resulted in substantial changes in the great travel flows and cross currents which have affected destinations differently. There has been a strong, fairly consistent growth in international travel since the 1960s with some hesitations in the 1970s following the energy crisis resulting in a quadrupling of the price of aviation fuel and depressed consumer demand. In the early 1980s there was another fall in the rate of growth following on world recession. Nevertheless, in the decade 1978–88 there has been an increase of 51 per cent in total arrivals, notwithstanding recession, political instability and exchange rates. For the coming ten years, growth is likely to average four per cent.

Table 3.1 International tourist arrivals

Year	Total (in millions)	% of the total number of arrivals				
		Europe	Americas	South- and East-Asia and Pacific Area	Africa	Middle-East
1950	25.3	66.6	29.6	0.9	2.1	0.8
1960	69.3	72.7	24.2	1.1	1.1	0.9
1965	112.7	74.2	20.6	1.8	1.3	2.1
1970	159.7	70.7	23.0	3.6	1.5	1.2
1975	214.4	71.8	20.1	4.3	2.2	1.6
1980	284.8	68.8	18.9	7.8	2.5	2.0
1985	325.7	66.9	18.0	9.3	3.0	2.8
1986	332.9	65.8	18.9	10.2	2.8	2.4
1987	358.7	65.2	18.9	10.8	2.8	2.3
1988[1]	390.0	64.5	18.6	11.5	3.1	2.3
1990*	421.8					
1995*	513.2					

Note: 1 Preliminary estimates
* Based on 1988: increased by 4% yearly from 1989 to 1995
Source: World Tourism Organization 1988.

The global picture has been mirrored by Europe, but Europe has suffered some loss of share. European destinations accounted for 72 per cent of world arrivals in 1975; by 1980 it had dropped to 69 per cent; by 1985 it had dropped further to 67 per cent, and in 1988 it was less than 65 per cent. It still retains its dominant position. North America has at best maintained its share, while Asia and the Pacific have improved performance dramatically over the past 25 years. Part of this is due to the rapid expansion in Japanese travel abroad since 1970. The Japanese Ten Million Programme met its target well ahead of time but the majority of first-time international travellers visit nearer South East Asian destinations.

These changes in travel flows arise for three reasons: changes in the market; changes at the destination and, not least, transport services between the two. Europeans are venturing further afield and those receiving countries such as Spain, Italy, Portugal and Greece, heavily reliant on intra-European travel, will need to diversify into new markets. Eastern Europe in the longer term could provide substantial markets, but significant earnings from these markets will not, it is felt, develop before the late 1990s because of the shortage of hard currency and their weak economies. There has been substantial investment in hotels, facilities and attractions in South East Asia and Australia which has attracted increased business. In some years some destinations in the Pacific basin have been *over hotelled* resulting in low prices, attractively priced packages and increased demand. This has been followed by high levels of room occupancy, increased prices, further investment.

In the short period since the Japanese outward travel movement started there has been massive development in air services and airports: Tokyo's Narita will be followed by Kansai International at Osaka which is scheduled for completion in 1993 and designed to handle 160,000 flights a year. Currently one of the great inhibitions to outbound Japanese travel is lack of aircraft capacity.

London's newest airport, Stansted, has recently become operational. Even so, a major handicap to the airline industry is congestion. IATA has recently launched an international campaign to publicise this. The proportion of delayed flights has almost doubled in the four years 1986–89 and it is forecast that sixteen European airports, including Heathrow, Gatwick and Manchester in Britain, and Frankfurt, Dusseldorf and Hamburg in Germany, will be capacity constrained by the year 2000. Not least it is forecast that Europe will run out of airspace by 2000 or even as early as 1995 unless the airspace map of Europe is redrawn.

Single Europe 1992 will result in liberalisation of air travel. This will open all major air routes to direct competition between airlines; provide stimulation for new routes to regional airports; and should result in some reduction in fares. Abolition of duty free shopping and the imposition of VAT on travel (currently zero rated) would have the opposite affect and increase prices. In 1993 there will be a Channel Tunnel. Trains will challenge aircraft on many prime European routes – London/Paris, London/Brussels. Will the balance be in favour of British travellers (especially from London and South East England) being syphoned off, or Britain as a destination tapping the potential not just of near European markets but also long haul travellers who visit Europe? Will the Tunnel help to grow Britain's incoming business, lose domestic business to Europe, or simply divert the travellers to another transport mode? The answer depends on marketing in its widest sense and related development. People do not travel simply because a new route opens. There is a trinity of forces; price, convenience/comfort, and trip satisfaction/fashion. An advantage in one of these alone will divert traffic, but to increase movement there must be an advantage in at least two of the three factors.

Socio-economic factors influence the generation and location of tourism. Time, desire to travel and income levels are the prerequisites. The most important factor, however, is likely to be the level of economic growth in those countries which are important generators of tourism traffic now or can be in the future. Economic forecasts suggest that the EC will benefit from the completion of the internal market in 1992. The official reports of the European Community forecast that the Community member countries' national incomes will rise between 2.5 and 7 per cent over the growth rates of the old separate national systems, a massive increase in prosperity. Two million extra jobs will be created and inflation will reduce by up to six per cent. Travel spending traditionally rises at twice the rate of GDP increases, or even more. Thus the potential for growth in the world's largest travel market is enormous. Growth will, however, be constrained to some extent by factors such as an ageing population and a relatively inflexible labour market. The most buoyant growth is expected to be in Southern European countries. Unemployment is expected to remain high in most European countries though the majority will have jobs and should continue to enjoy increasing disposable incomes. Social trends continue to favour spending rather than saving. Economies in many Asian countries should continue to strengthen. The American market will continue to offer huge potential.

Opportunities exist in market segments as well as geographic markets: the senior citizen with disposable income, the will and the ability to indulge in international travel; the youth market with its anxiety to succeed, to learn new skills essential for success; the special interest traveller; the business traveller.

Demographic trends

Among the more important macro-trends vitally important to tourism are the demographic ones such as population growth, life expectancy and age profile. The populations of both Canada and the USA will show moderate growth, forecasts suggest by about a fifth between 1985 and 2010. The proportion of the population up to age 14 will remain fairly static, while retired people (64 plus) will account for a larger share of total population. By 1995 about one in eight of Americans will be senior citizens. Populations of Latin American countries are expected to grow twice as fast: the 0–14 years range will continue to account for more than a third of the population, while only about one in twenty will be over 64.

Asia (excluding Japan) is expected to have much larger populations – in some cases doubling between 1985 and 2010. About a third of these populations will be under 14 years, while people over 64 will represent a very small proportion of the total population – much the same pattern as predicated for Latin America. Japan is the most rapidly ageing population in the world

– one in ten were over 64 years old in 1985 and this is forecast to increase to just over one in seven by 2010. The percentage of the Japanese population younger than fourteen is forecast to decrease from 21.8 per cent in 1985 to 18.2 per cent in 1995.

The population of Australia is predicated to grow modestly (23.6 per cent between 1985 and 2010) and again there will be a shift in the age profile – an increase in seniors and a decrease in those less than fourteen.

In the Middle East and Africa, population growth is likely to be spectacular – doubling or even trebling in some cases. However famine, war and AIDs could well be nature's answer to a population explosion which would be difficult to sustain. The population of Kenya for example is currently predicted to grow from just over 20 million in 1985 to nearly 56 million in 2010.

Undoubtedly Europe will continue to dominate the international travel picture in the foreseeable future. Practically all Western Europeans enjoy above average standards of living when compared with world standards. There are significant populations in Eastern Europe emerging from Communism with its centralised controls but who are not yet significant as potential international travellers. Furthermore there are significant proportions of populations in Eastern Europe whose priorities as consumers do not match those of developed countries, eg about 60 million Muslims in Turkey and Yugoslavia. Religions and political ideologies are important factors in interpreting demographic trends.

The population of the European Community is growing very slowly. Indeed the populations of Belgium, Denmark, Germany and Italy are declining. Only in Ireland and Portugal are populations forecast to grow in double figures between 1985 and 2010. Birthrates in Western Europe have fallen as a result of economic recession, increasingly sophisticated expectations and easier abortion. The drop in birthrate during the 1970s recession years will have a significant impact in the next two decades. According to EC forecasts, the number of EC residents between 15 and 25 years will fall by 15 per cent between 1985 and 1995 with higher than average falls in Germany, Scandinavia, the United Kingdom and Benelux countries. In the short term the 25 to 45 year old age group will increase in size between now and 1995. While this is an affluent sector at the peak of their earning power, there are many demands on these earnings with families growing up. However couples are tending to postpone marriage and the start of families. The average child bearing age is increasing in Western Europe (except in Ireland, Greece and Portugal) as well as in Eastern Europe. Western Europe has an older population profile than any other continent.

By the end of the century one in four Europeans will be over the age of 55. Improved standards of medicine have raised life expectancy for both males and females – the average age of death has increased by about ten years since 1945. This increasingly healthy and longer living segment is also tending to retire earlier from their working careers, either because of the pressures of unemployment or because increasingly caring and affluent societies felt that the elderly should not have to work so long. In 1988 the average legal retirement age for males in Western Europe was 62.5 years and for females 58 years. The biggest changes in the 1990s will be record numbers of senior citizens not only in Europe but in most developed countries in the world. It is this mature and concerned segment, increasingly active in green issues and preoccupied with lifestyle, which is already impacting on tourism management.

On the other hand, all over Europe there will be far fewer young people, but about one in five of them will go on to higher education. The fall in the birthrate in the 1970s will result in far fewer teenagers in 1995. At the same time the number of jobs in Europe demanding cerebral skills is increasing, while those demanding manual skills is declining. The Warwick Institute for Employment Research estimated that of 1.7 million new jobs expected in Britain by 1995, one million will be professional or equivalent while 400,000 manual jobs will have disappeared by then. This pattern will be mirrored in other Western European countries. Competition for the better educated will intensify and there will be an increased incentive to be better educated.

In Russia, Turkey and Yugoslavia the increases in population have been largely among the Muslim peoples. For example, for the first time since 1915 the Russians now comprise less than half of the population of the USSR, since the population growth has been among the Muslims of the Southern Republics.

Table 3.2 shows the forecasts for population growth in significant markets for international travel and other countries where, if economies strengthen substantially, growth could be explosive.

Is it economically viable?

In the past year or so we have seen tour operators dropping Spanish, Turkish and other European hotels from their programmes because standards are simply not high enough to meet the needs of today's increasingly sophisticated traveller. As people travel further afield they are exposed to standards of accommodation and levels of service in Asia and America which cause them to revise their expectations about standards in some of our European cities and resorts. As expectations increase the tourism providers need to improve and adapt to meet these expectations. Increasingly there is a demand for higher standards but above all value for money.

Table 3.2 Demographic trends and forecast – selected countries

	'000 Actual 1985	'000 1990	'000 2000	'000 2010	% Change 1985–2010	Population 0–14 1985 %	Population 0–14 1995 %	Population +64 1985 %	Population +64 1995 %
Canada	25426	26746	28927	30739	+20.9	21.5	20.9	10.4	11.9
USA	238020	248429	286239	286294	+20.3	21.9	22.4	11.7	12.3
North America	263446	275175	297166	317033	+20.3	21.7	21.6	11.0	12.1
Brazil	135564	150368	179487	207454	+53.0	36.4	33.7	4.3	5.1
Mexico	78996	89012	109180	128241	+62.3	42.2	36.5	3.5	3.9
Colombia	28714	31820	37999	43840	+52.7	37.2	34.7	5.7	6.5
India	758927	827152	964072	1086344	+43.1	36.8	32.3	4.3	5.1
Japan	120742	123865	129725	133049	+10.2	21.8	18.2	10.0	13.2
Indonesia	166440	181539	211367	238605	+43.4	38.7	33.4	3.5	4.3
China	na	na	na	na	na	na	na	na	na
S. Korea	41258	44828	50961	55942	+35.6	31.2	28.6	4.0	5.0
Australia	15698	16708	18628	20319	+29.4	23.6	22.2	10.1	11.2
New Zealand	3318	3464	3749	3968	+19.6	24.1	22.1	10.4	11.1
Egypt	46909	52536	63941	75263	+67.6	39.6	36.7	4.0	4.2
Iran	44632	51529	65161	79044	+77.1	42.7	39.8	3.3	3.4
Iraq	15898	18760	25377	32866	+106.7	46.9	44.1	2.7	2.9
Saudi Arabia	11542	13988	19824	26937	+133.8	44.6	44.2	2.6	2.6
Syria	10505	12634	17809	23284	+121.6	48.3	48.0	2.7	2.6
Kenya	20600	25413	38534	55801	+170.9	52.5	52.4	1.8	1.8
S. Africa	32392	36754	46918	58525	+80.7	41.0	40.9	4.0	4.0
Belgium	9857	9785	9666	9406	–4.6	19.0	18.1	13.7	16.0
Denmark	5111	5099	5114	5019	–1.8	18.6	16.6	15.0	15.7
France	55062	55475	57162	57929	+5.2	21.3	19.9	12.8	13.8
Germany FDR & GDR	77720	77221	76633	74631	+4.0	16.0	16.8	15.1	15.2
Greece	9919	9880	10435	10523	+6.1	21.1	23	13.3	13.6
Ireland	3540	3843	4320	4759	+34.4	29.5	28.4	10.6	9.5
Italy	57080	57379	57375	55800	–2.2	19.5	16.1	12.7	15.9
Luxembourg	366	370	374	369	+0.8	17.2	19.0	13.1	13.1
Netherlands	14454	14777	15213	15148	+4.8	19.7	17.6	12.0	13.6
Portugal	10129	10497	11141	11423	+12.8	23.8	19.7	11.9	13.2
Spain	38495	39241	40691	41205	+7.0	23.6	19.1	11.9	14.1
United Kingdom	56618	57291	58859	59500	+5.1	19.4	19.9	15.0	15.8
Total EC (INC. GDR)	338351	340858	346983	345712	+2.2	19.7	18.4	13.6	14.8

Table 3.2 Demographic trends and forecast – selected countries (continued)

	'000 Actual	'000	'000	'000	% Change	Population 0–14		Population +64	
	1985	1990	2000	2010	1985–2010	1985 %	1995 %	1985 %	1995 %
Austria	7558	7587	7628	7537	-0.3	18.2	17.4	14.3	15.7
Findland	4894	5006	5073	5048	+3.1	19.4	18.6	12.4	14.5
Iceland	241	250	262	272	+12.9	26.1	22.3	10.0	11.3
Norway	4146	4214	4319	4346	+4.8	20.1	18.3	15.6	16.4
Sweden	8343	8442	8539	8514	+2.0	18.2	17.7	17.0	17.9
Switzerland	6456	6485	6438	6430	-0.4	17.	16.2	14.0	15.6
Total EFTA	31638	31984	32259	32147	+1.6	18.6	17.6	14.8	16.2
Poland	37063	38513	40816	42943	+15.9	na	23.8	na	11.1
USSR	277537	291822	314736	337120	+21.5	24.8	23.7	9.3	11.0
Turkey	50306	56941	73029	93000	+84.9	na	33.5	na	4.9
Yugoslavia	23118	24107	25653	28050	+21.3	na	21.2	na	10.9

Note: na = not available
Source: Euromonitor International Marketing 13 Edition 1988/9
U.N. World Population Prospects/National Statistical offices.

As we approach Single Europe customer expectations will continue to grow. The *Package Travel Directive* was adopted in June 1990 and should become law in all member states by 31 December 1992. It is designed to provide consumer protection to those who have bought packaged holidays by ensuring that they get compensation when things go wrong by imposing precise liability on organisers. In future, tour operators and travel agents will have to accept legal responsibility for the services (accommodation, travel etc) they offer. Exceptions will be made where there are unforeseen circumstances impossible to overcome but even then organisers must give all possible assistance to clients. Statements and claims made in the brochure will be binding on the operator or retailer and there are stringent conditions relative to price. It follows then that the operator will look to the provider of the product to ensure the highest possible quality relative to price and to deliver a product of the highest possible standard providing value for money.

Today's traveller is very different from the traveller of the 1950s and 1960s. Tomorrow's traveller will have even higher expectations, the provision of which needs to be economically viable.

Is it socially compatible?

The rapid expansion of tourism over the last thirty years or so has impinged on cultures and lifestyles and in turn has given rise to social problems. Too often economic aid from wealthier nations to poorer ones had been used to finance tourism developments without too much thought given to the social or environmental fabric of the destination. Tourism was seen as a panacea for economic problems, for trade imbalances or for unemployment but planners and developers did not take account of the social implications. In extreme cases the local population has been exploited by unscrupulous businessmen. In Thailand there is male and female prostitution in the main tourist resorts. A few years ago substantial numbers of Japanese males undertook sex tours to South East Asia. The experience of the last thirty years though has resulted in an awareness at least of the social pressures which can develop; an understanding of the potential social problems and hopefully an improved planning regime; training and management of tourism developments. Governments or their agencies at both national and local levels will undertake strategic planning of the tourism sector which will address such factors as social pressures in the development of guidelines for the industry. It will no longer be enough for governments to determine tourism development solely on the basis of economic criteria. Social and environmental issues will also need to be addressed. This will determine, for example, whether to go for mass tourism, or the independent traveller; the rate of growth; the roles of the public and private sectors; the level of incentives; legislation; investment in infrastructure and training.

Socially compatible is capable of another interpretation – that of providing for special needs. The Holiday Care Service is the United Kingdom's central source of holiday information for people whose age, disability or other personal or family circumstances affect their choice of holiday. Under its Chairman, Mary Baker, a working party was set up to make recommendations for action by the industry over the next ten years. The working party's report was published in 1989:

> We consider that there has to be much more provision for people with special needs in mainstream holiday-taking. While there will continue to be a role for the many excellent facilities, often run by charities, that exist for group or individual holidays for those with a particular disability, we hope the tourism industry as a whole will adopt the Tourism for All philosophy of aiming to cater for everyone's needs. To include and not to segregate. Accessibility, in its widest sense, should

> be seen as an integral part of excellent service. The statement often expressed to us, that a person is not handicapped by their disability but by the environment, should be taken to heart by the tourism industry.[1]

A caring society will be increasingly concerned to ensure that the disadvantaged are enabled to take holidays.

Is it environmentally acceptable?

Green issues are increasingly a permanent item on the political agenda of national and local governments. Tourism development, like other developments, must be politically acceptable, socially responsible and environmentally sound. The new catch phrase is *responsible tourism* or *sustainable tourism*. Lane said:

> Neither the French term *tourism doux* nor the German *sanfter tourismus* translates well into English, although the translation *soft tourism* has been commonly used with mixed results. *Green tourism* and *alternative tourism* have slightly wholefood connotations, while *responsible tourism* sounds drearily worthy. *Post industrial tourism* is fine for specialists, but confuses the public. *Sustainable tourism* captures the image of the long term goal, an ability to sustain host area, holiday maker and operators alike.[2]

He goes on to suggest that tourism development should be gradual and organic; should provide for economic growth without dominating the economy; and should not abuse the natural environment. While environmental issues are becoming popular and thus politically interesting, much of the comment and study tends to be either very academic or theoretical, eg soft tourism, alternative tourism, ecotourism, reflecting the interest of the commentator, rather than practical. The trades are vitally concerned. Government cannot act alone. Restriction of traffic and control may not be the right answer but rather creative planning and expansion which needs the collective effort of operators and controllers. Award schemes and other motivating programmes affecting the providers and the tourists themselves are important. One of the most successful examples of this is the Blue Flag clean beach programme, which is not dependent on statutory order. This has done more than direct Government order to deal with an important aspect of tourism provision.

While this may seem idealistic, the English Tourist Board together with the Countryside Commission and The Rural Development Commission recently organised the first national conference on the subject – *Shades of Green*. In fact the idea of *sustainable* tourism was first mooted in Switzerland as an antidote to the environmental damage being caused in the Alps by the skilling industry. It is not cheap, it needs a responsible approach, careful management and controlled planning, creative and selective marketing, education and training. It will be increasingly important – a major political issue of the 1990s.

Climate change and its impact

Ultimately tourism is dependent on environmental factors and these resources are in turn dependent on climatic conditions. A significant change in world climate would impact on travel patterns and should certainly feature in the planning of tourism product development. Mediterranean beaches and Alpine ski resorts are sensitive to climatic conditions and dependent on the right conditions for success. We read much about the greenhouse effect, of melting polar icecaps and global warming and we have seen some evidence in recent years of changing patterns of weather. Britain enjoyed two successive hot summers in 1989 and 1990 and this has impacted on holidays at home though there are arguably other reasons for Britons holidaying in British as opposed to Mediterranean or Adriatic resorts. Certainly there is a correlation between poor summers in Northern Europe and residents of Northern Europe holidaying at a sun resort the following year. A poor summer at home persuades more residents to holiday in the Mediterranean the following year. At present one third of all tourist arrivals throughout the world are in the Mediterranean region. This success had its beginnings more than a century ago. Easier and cheaper travel, massive investment in infrastructure and accommodation, marketing initiatives, growing affluence in source markets and fashion, all accelerated the growth. By the end of the century the attractions of the Mediterranean resorts may well have reduced if there is a continuation of hot summers in Northern Europe.

Conversely some of the ski resorts of Canada and California, the Alps and the Pyrenees may well find that within a couple of decades they enjoy a less viable winter sports season. The 1988/89 winter was disastrous for Scotland's winter sports. Rising water levels are already threatening Venice and could well affect waterfront developments such as marinas and beaches, and some areas and low lying islands may disappear altogether.

Climatic changes would affect seasonality. Northern Italian resorts could find that their high season was in the winter months while Southern England's resorts enjoyed a long summer season.

Increasingly though we are seeing climate controlled resorts such as Centre Parc in Sherwood Forest or Sandcastle in Blackpool. We are also seeing significant progress in snow making machines designed to provide *designer* snow in snowless winter sports resorts.

There are several schools of thought about the greenhouse effect and global warming, how quickly it will accelerate and how effectively it can be retarded. How will trends develop and interact? It is doubtful if forecasting, or attempting to forecast climatic change would be very productive at this stage. One thing is certain though, tourism is climate sensitive and significant changes in the world's weather would significantly impact on tourism demand. It is equally doubtful if climate can be artificially controlled on a massive scale. K. Smith of Stirling University says:

> Tourism and recreation will react sharply to all the economic, social and technological changes which are likely to take place in the future. Many of these may override the consequences of climatic change. Therefore the best way forward is probably through a strategy which links a better understanding of the present weather and climate sensitivity of tourism with the improved predictions which will come over the next few years from the numerical models.[3]

Climatic changes however tend to be very long term influences, and it is by no means certain that contemporary fluctuations, surprising as they may be, will have permanent effects in the next two decades or so. Change is more likely to come from fashion or marketing activity. In the past hundred years winter resorts have become summer resorts (the Mediterranean and North Africa). Nowhere is too hot. In Northern Europe most people no longer bathe in the sea. Seafront hotels must have swimming pools. In Britain the spas as medical centres have died. City hotels (London for example) are full at weekends. The main resorts hotels' low season is August. Such major changes in traffic are a few examples of the power of changing trends, lifestyles and marketing action. The power to cause such change and the speed with which it can be done have never been greater.

References

1 *Tourism for All* A report of the working party chaired by Mary Baker. English Tourist Board in association with The Holiday Care Service, Scottish Tourist Board, Wales Tourist Board 1989. p 14

2 Lane B. *A seminar on Tourism and the Environment* University of Bristol. London, June 1990

3 Smith K. *Tourism and Climatic Change. Land Use Policy.* April 1990. p 180.

4 Reading the trends

Chapter 2 traced a short history of tourism and looked at some of the markets, segments and trends which are beginning to emerge. Demographics play a large part in tourism as does the availability of leisure time and disposable income.

Specialisation and demand for quality are also beginning to manifest themselves. As for the industry, there is a perceptible polarisation of businesses into larger and larger groupings – transporters and hotel groups or even consortia, tour operators and retailers. The European Single Market 1992 is likely to see further acceleration of polarisation. Already about half of the population of Britain might be called *green consumers* and by far the majority are concerned about environmental issues. All political parties are having to take this on board in formulating their policies. It is not just Britain, it is a world wide phenomenon and tourism and leisure will not be exempt from these policies. Single Europe will also see liberalisation of intra-European air routes and fares; liberalisation of coach travel; harmonisation of VAT rates; more consumer protection for those buying packaged holidays within the Community; and free movement of labour. The Channel Tunnel is planned to open in 1993. There are unprecedented developments in Eastern Europe and healthy economies emerging in Asia – markets of the future – but tourist destinations of today.

Markets for the future

While Europe has lost share of world travel movements, dropping from 72 per cent in 1975 to less than 65 per cent in 1988, it has nevertheless maintained its dominant position. The population of the European Community is growing very slowly but Single Europe and major transport improvements will encourage more intra-European travel in the years up to the end of the century by which time Eastern European markets may well be developing strongly.

The pace of political change has been extremely rapid in 1989 and 1990:

June 1989	A new Solidarity government elected in Poland.
April 1990	Democratic governments elected in Slovenia and Croatia.
May 1990	A centre left government installed in Hungary.
June 1990	Czechoslovakia moves to multi-party democracy. In Bulgaria, the Communist party retain power following relatively free elections. National Salvation Front elected in Romania.
July 1990	28th Communist Party Congress enhanced Mr. Gorbachev's presidential role.
October 1990	Reunification of Germany.

These countries which have been through a period of rapid political change are now espousing the virtues of free market economies. But while political reform can be achieved relatively quickly, industrial and economic reform is rather more uncertain and certainly has a much longer timescale. It will be some time before healthy stable foreign exchange positions have been built up. As substantial generators of tourist traffic we need to look perhaps a decade ahead.

Eastern European countries are already becoming receivers of tourist traffic which will impact increasingly on existing destinations. There are many second and third generation Eastern Europeans who are now nationals of North America or Western European countries and they are already visiting friends and relatives in Eastern Europe, finding their roots. Undoubtedly Eastern Europe will syphon off traffic even in the short term. However, in the medium to long term these countries will provide stiff competition for those destinations offering cultural and rural tourism. There is, in most cases, a rich cultural heritage (128 concert halls and 88 state orchestras existed in East Germany and there are in excess of 3,000 castles in Czechoslovakia). There is a dearth of beds – Prague has only 10,000; an antiquated and inadequate telecommunications network; and a poor transport system. Market demand already exists. A great curiosity value attaches to the region. Tourism is a potential foreign currency earner and once developed this in turn will create outbound traffic from the region. Hungary's trade minister predicts that by the year 2000 tourism will be the country's most lucrative industry.

The real potential for travel out of the region will not be realised from some years but already outbound travel is increasing faster than the world average, albeit from small bases. It seems likely that

Poland, Yugoslavia, Hungary and Czechoslovakia will realise their tourism potential ahead of the other countries of Eastern Europe.

Japan is already a recognised force in the field of international tourism. The Japanese Ten Million Programme met its target way ahead of time and it is already fourth in the world league table of visitor spend. The newly industrialised countries of Asia (Singapore, Taiwan, India, Thailand and South Korea) are already beginning to generate substantial numbers of international travellers and they tend to be high spenders. These countries are also beginning to invest in tourism: the Hong Kong based Park Lane International has recently bought London's Churchill Hotel; Nicko International, Taj International and Seibu Saison are among groups with equity in London properties; the Sultan of Brunei owns London's Dorchester Hotel. This phenomenon is not restricted to London or even Europe. Asian money is being invested in tourism plant in the Americas, Australia, and now Eastern Europe as well as in Asia itself.

The majority of US travel is domestic. It is estimated that as much as 97 per cent is domestic. Just over 40 million people made international trips in 1989 and this includes non-passport trips to Mexico and Canada. Indeed, only about 10 per cent of Americans have a passport. Following US deregulation of America's airline system in 1978 there was a substantial increase in the air travel market stimulated by low fares. This has encouraged holidays at home and as a result outbound travel has increased slowly over the past few years, apart from travel to Mexico which has increased by more than 30 per cent since 1985. Between 1985 and 1989 there was 18 per cent increase in Americans travelling to overseas destinations. Rates of increase varied from Central America and Australasia – both increased over 60 per cent to Europe which only increased 8 per cent over this period. Leisure travel dominates both domestic and international travel.

Outbound travel by Americans will continue to be affected by the US economy, travel costs, exchange rates and, not least, the world political situation. Perhaps the most significant factor for outgoing American travel is the greying of the population which should provide a significant impetus to foreign travel over the next two decades. There is no statutory retirement age for Americans and there is a trend to longer, not shorter, working weeks. Holiday entitlement is only two to three weeks compared with the Netherlands and West Germany where it is currently seven or eight weeks. In Japan it is still only two weeks. of which only about eight days is taken. It could well be that in another twenty years, ten weeks annual holiday will be the norm. People will be more concerned with increased leisure time than increased salaries. Just as there will be more concern over environmental issues and a better quality of life than an increased standard of living. Certainly holiday entitlements in the USA and Japan must increase to be more in line with those currently enjoyed by Europeans.

The Economist Intelligence Unit (EIU) expects the growth in international travel to moderate between now and the end of the century with the greatest expansion from Japan and Europe, and a decline in international travel by US residents. A recent European Travel Commission (ETC) study on the other hand suggested that the current traffic to Europe of about six million represents only about one fifth of the target audience.

The Working Group of Research Directors in the European Travel Commission identified the following megatrends for tourism in the next decade:

1. Global travel spending and particularly transport spending in, into and from Europe will increase faster than other budget items, due to more frequent, albeit shorter, holidays. Although daily expenditure will generally be maintained due to higher quality requirements, average expenditure per trips may decrease due to shorter duration of holidays.
2. Long haul holidays to and from Europe will increase faster than intra-European vacation holidays, to and from practically all the continents, notably America, Asia and Oceania.
3. With Europe, city travel will increase faster than summer and beach vacation holidays, due to parallel and steady increases of both *short breaks* with cultural or pseudo-cultural motivations and all forms of *business travel*, e.g. incentives, conventions, conferences, also exhibitions and fairs.
4. South-north, east-west and west-east travel will increase relatively faster than traditional north-south holidays, although their figures are still much lower.
5. Traffic across the present intra-European borders will increase faster than domestic travel in most European countries.
6. Winter sunshine holidays, cultural winter tours and cruises will increase faster than winter sports holidays.
7. Air traffic, both short and long haul, will still increase faster than other types of transportation due to various factors including new direct connections, although other means of transport will also show growth, including new convenient rail links.
8. Inclusive travel will grow faster than independent travel in spite of price increases justified by selecting generally higher quality packages and accommodation and/or farther destinations.
9. Hotel accommodation of all levels will gain more customers than

other types of accommodation, with more growth for higher class hotels in resorts and more growth for economy hotels in cities.

10. Late reservations will increase faster than early bookings and the role of CRS systems will increase.
11. Two age groups will increase faster than others; senior citizens (due *inter alia* to growing numbers and increased means of pensioners) and young people (due to increased education and new travel opportunities).
12. As a consequence both the demand for cultural visits and cultural holidays, and for active summer/winter holidays will grow faster than other form of vacation.
13. Groups including families will tend to be smaller and more flexible.

Segments with potential

The demographic picture (*see* Chapter 3) suggests that *youth* tourism and above all senior citizen travel will increase much more rapidly than that of the working population though business travel (especially incentive and conference traffic) should continue to show a healthy increase.

There is perhaps a correlation between the greying of populations in developed countries and concern over environmental issues. There is much new interest in rural tourism, farm tourism, special interest tourism, as well as walking and activity holidays. It is increasingly about slimming bodies and broadening minds. Senior citizens are sensitive to security so comfort and developments will need to reflect their needs. Furthermore, higher educational levels are accompanied by increased sophistication and a heightened sense of comfort. The youth market, despite their decreasing share of total populations in tourism generating countries, will continue to travel and this will be further facilitated in 1993 when Europe will be *sans frontieres*. They will continue to travel in their quest for skills and study. English language study will be a powerful motivator.

Thanks largely to third age tourists, seasonality will tend to be less pronounced and there will be a better spread of travel throughout the year. Increasingly the third age is seen as a time for living.

More and more people will be leaving full-time employment in their fifties, in part because they no longer want to have the pressures but in part because they will vacate it to allow younger, more energetic and perhaps better qualified colleagues to take over. These early retirees may well take on part-time or voluntary work, and they will have much more leisure time at their disposal.

Lifestyle is already beginning to change quite rapidly: more concern for health resulting in an increase in membership of leisure clubs and an increase in activity holidays – walking, cycling, golfing; more concern with self improvement and self expression as evidenced in increased uptake of adult evening courses and leisure learning weekends as well as special interest holidays. Both trends will accelerate over the next decade.

The growth of international business travel has been sustained even in times of recession. Arguably there is more need to travel when there is recession to secure new business. Improved communications and teleconferencing has not seen a decline in the need for face to face communication. This is especially true of conference traffic. Similarly there is a long established travel movement to visit trade fairs and exhibitions. In recent years growth has been substantial but there is still a very large potential. Single Europe, sometimes regarded as *Fortress Europe* by third world countries will produce more business travel both on an intra-European and intercontinental basis. Business travel should continue to be a very resilient growth segment with opportunities for additional business from *extenders* – those who can be persuaded to add a leisure break to a business trip, and accompanying spouse travel.

Green tourism

Outdoor activities are growing in popularity, demand for rural holidays and farm holidays is increasing. It seems certain that tourism providers will increasingly have to meet the needs of a much more environmentally aware traveller. Planning applications will undoubtedly come under closer scrutiny. Energy conservation, architectural design which blends unobtrusively, materials used in construction which are *green* will all be called for by an ever more environmentally aware traveller and consumer.

Destinations which offer a clean, attractive environment will have a substantial advantage in the future. Environmental concerns will affect decisions about tourist destinations. The environment is a key tourism resource.

> Environmental impact is a major concern in the development of tourism projects. Lack of attention to the possible impacts may lead to the degradation of the very resources on which tourism is based. Equally however tourism development can have a positive impact, particularly on the built environment through the upgrading of buildings

> and provision of infrastructure. It is apparent that if tourism agencies and developers involved in tourism projects are to assess the environmental impact of their proposals quickly, cheap, yet reliable methods of assessment are needed.
>
> The utilisation of the Delphi technique represents one such approach.[1]

Indeed the dependence of tourism on quality natural resources makes environmentally caring policies economically sound policies. Furthermore, increasing leisure time, at least in Europe, will mean that tourism developments will increasingly need to cater for the leisure need of the local population as well as the incoming tourist. Local people will thus have a say in developments and therefore environmental issues. The World Bank and the World Tourism Organisation (WTO) both argue strongly for environmentally sound development as do an increasing number of national tourist organisations.

Tourism developments will need to be aware of consumer expectations, changing demographics and life styles. How will the industry respond to the challenge?

Transporters

The European Council of Ministers has agreed to deregulation. It was the airline industry which triggered the growth of mass tourism to the Mediterranean in the late 1950s. It was as a direct consequence that new resorts like Lloret de Mar and Torremolinos exploded on the scene. Airline deregulation in the US caused the massive expansion in domestic air travel to the point where almost 80 per cent of US adults in 1989 had flown at one time or another in their lives. From January 1993 European governments will no longer be able to guarantee national carriers a fixed percentage of capacity on a route. Already some routes have been deregulated – for example London and Dublin, which was served by Aer Lingus and British Airways, until 1986 when the Irish airline Ryanair began flights from London to Luton. Subsequently this group was joined by Virgin Atlantic. Flight frequencies have increased and prices for leisure travellers have fallen. This will be replicated on other routes. But there is increasing pressure on airspace and congestion at airports. It is forecast that 16 European airports will be capacity constrained by the end of the century (see Chapter 3). Strong growth in the leisure market will ensure increased demand for travel but the method of travel will be dependent on the ability of the transporter to meet the fare expectations of the future. Competition, especially in Europe, from other forms of travel will intensify. It has been clearly demonstrated many times in the past that if fares fall demand for air travel increases. The constraint to lower prices and increased demand from leisure travellers lies in the price of aviation fuel and the uncertainty attaching to the oil producing countries. It seems likely though that there will be continuing innovation in the fare structures offered by the airline industry in getting the right yield balance from the right mix of business and leisure travellers.

Michael Downe, aerospace correspondent of *The Financial Times*, wrote:

> Already vast sums are being spent in an attempt to rectify the air traffic control deficiencies that have arisen in recent years, especially in Western Europe. At the same time vast sums are being spent or earmarked to bring other elements of the ground infrastructure up to date. It has been estimated that worldwide some $150 billion will be spent by the end of the century on modernising and expanding the airports system, together with associated road and rail access links, to enable it to cope with the rising tide of traffic.[2]

In Europe there will be additional competition from the Channel Tunnel, scheduled to be completed in 1993. This could well result in a price war which will stimulate business in North West Europe particularly, including the southern part of Britain. The speed with which the high speed trains together with the Tunnel link will carry passengers from city centre to city centre will be an important factor in the equation.

> For passenger flows from the centre of London to the centre of Paris or Brussels rail will be more competitive than air for both time and price. At longer distances however air is more competitive since end to end journey times do not increase in the same way as they do by rail. Furthermore, the cost structure of airline operations favours longer haul flights as against short haul operations.[3]

While there will be some transfer of traffic from existing forms of transport – air and sea – to the new international passenger services by rail, the market will undoubtedly grow as the quality of travel improves, prices reduce in real terms and lifestyles change. The Channel Tunnel also removes the water barrier between Britain and the rest of the Continent, which has been a deterrent for some travellers. The Northern European markets of Britain, Benelux, France and Germany are not the only ones offering potential. Markets further afield – Switzerland, Spain and Italy – for Britain will undoubtedly use the Tunnel for car-borne holidays and even Americans and Japanese undertaking a European tour. While punctuality is perhaps not such an important factor for the leisure traveller it undoubtedly is for the business traveller. It will be difficult for the airlines to match the punctuality offered by the train without a substantial overhaul of traffic control systems.

There is a transport revolution taking place in Europe. In France ten times as many passengers take the Train de Grande Vitesse (TGV) as fly the 300 miles from Paris to Lyons. Further TGV routes are being developed – Paris – Brittany, a northern route to Brussels and beyond, a Channel Tunnel link, a south-western service. Italy's state railway plans 2,200 kilometres for its Alta Velocita network. German Federal Railways plans two north – south links joined with an east – west route. In Spain, Madrid – Cordoba – Seville is planned for completion in 1992 with a Madrid – Saragossa – Barcelona link coming later. British Rail plan additional capacity for the London – Tunnel link by the end of the century and international terminals at Waterloo and Kings Cross which will link with the InterCity system. In Europe there is something of a railway renaissance.

In the meantime the ferry companies have not been idle. There has been substantial investment in new ships and much more attention given to segmentation of passengers in comfortable, well designed accommodation. The ferry crossing is increasingly being positioned as part of the holiday.

Governments must recognise that if they are to secure the economic benefits which derive from tourism they must invest in the infrastructure and receptive services. Governments in the Far East have recognised the need to invest in airport developments – Singapore, Malaysia, Thailand and Taiwan – and market demand has been matched by a growth in services by the airlines with a growth rate far higher than Europe and the USA. In Hong Kong and Japan however, because of space problems and social pressure, constraints are being placed on the development of markets.

Accommodation providers

The *green revolution* will also impinge on the whole accommodation sector as will demographics. Segmentation will become even more important. Marketing will be the key to success and so there will be large groups, more co-operative marketing undertaken by consortia, more branding. Not least in importance over the next decade will be the emergence of new markets and new destinations. Seasonality is now a marketing opportunity rather than a problem. Seasonality remains a major challenge since 50 per cent of the accommodation capacity in Europe is unused over the year. However there is the possibility of dramatic change.

Hoteliers and other accommodation providers need to be aware of changing consumer demands as well as the opportunities offered by faster and more frequent transport services. The generation coming up, unlike the one before, has grown up with many experiences of staying in hotels. They are as a consequence more demanding, more discerning and more sophisticated. At the same time there is the senior citizen with the disposable income and the desire to travel, and the business executive – increasingly a woman. The market is highly fragmented; segmentation is the name of the game and each segment's needs must be identified and provided for. Significant changes are taking place and it behoves the accommodation providers to be aware of them.

The British Tourist Authority has published guidelines for the industry interested in developing business from the burgeoning Japanese market – *Caring for the Japanese Visitor.* This is symptomatic of the need to target ethnic and cultural, even religious, groups in the marketing, product development and product presentation by the hotels and restaurants sectors in the future. The hotel of the future will be more focused on particular market segments and at the same time will recognise the enormous interest and concern about environmental matters, health and self fulfillment. There will undoubtedly be a tendency for shorter stays, arising from short break leisure trips, and an increase in the share accounted for by business trips. There has been a trend for the leisure traveller increasingly to holiday in self catering accommodation, holiday villages, or even second homes. Hoteliers may well have to respond to this trend in the same way that the airlines have with a complex tariff structure.

It is already happening in city centre hotels throughout the world with its equivalent of business class – the executive floors. More than 50 per cent of most hotels' occupancy comes from business travellers but this tends to leave weekends with low occupancy levels unless something is done to attract additional business. This could be that same business traveller extending his stay to include a leisure break or more likely a leisure traveller. The needs of the business traveller will continue to be paramount and so health and fitness facilities are here to stay and there will be more and more demand for non-smoking rooms or floors; women only floors with dedicated lift service; or even women only hotels to meet the needs of the increasing number of female business executives. In the USA almost 40 per cent of all business executives are female.

Not all business travellers have an unlimited budget. This is certainly true of the leisure traveller who wishes to stay in hotels. So there will be increasing branding of hotel products to cater for different budget brackets. There will also be more niche marketing appealing to one particular market segment. This will particularly appeal to the small groups while it is more likely that the larger ones, such as Trusthouse Forte, will brand across the price range. Chains with sufficient stock have developed several brands – luxury, core and economy or budget sectors.

There will be more segmentation within the business travel sector too. The size of incentive groups is already getting smaller and it seems probable that organisers of groups of say 10 or 30 couples will want to take over the whole of a small hotel in order to develop a house party atmosphere with *built-in* entertainment such as we see currently aimed at the leisure market with music or antique appreciation weekends. The conference and meetings market will continue to expand and their needs will be increasingly sophisticated.

Already a large number of people are vegetarian and their numbers are growing. Top hotels like London's Ritz have had vegetarian dishes on their menus for some time. Any business group, be it incentive or conference, is likely to have at least one, and probably more, vegetarians and if the hotel cannot cope it will lose the business.

Environmental issues will affect the design of hotels; noise pollution, energy conservation, hygiene. Increased segmentation of the market will also affect design: guest safety, especially for elderly and women guests, will be important. Crest Hotels in Britain launched its *Lady Crest* rooms in 1983, which provided irons and ironing boards, skirt hangers and make up mirrors, as well as hairdryers, toiletries and bathrobes.

Asian hotels consistently feature in the *world's best* league tables and groups like the Hong Kong based Mandarin Oriental and Regent International groups, The Taj, New World Hotels, Park Lane Hotels and Regal Hotels, are looking to expand into America and Europe and they will set new standards for service and design. The opening up of Eastern Europe has provoked an unprecedented demand for more hotel accommodation of a standard high enough to attract the international traveller. Many hoteliers are alive to this demand. Trusthouse Forte has already agreed to renovate and manage The Bristol in Warsaw. The hotel industry is on the move.

Technology

Computer Reservation Systems (CRS), video, fax, personal computers – the effects of the new technology moves us inexorably towards the instant customised holiday. Only those destinations and services which have the technology will benefit from the increasing trend to shorter gestation between planning and decision. There will be a much shorter lead time and those with the technology will not only gain in this way but will be able to reduce costs. Tomorrow's traveller will be a child of the information technology age.

Making it *easy to buy* is a most important but much neglected marketing requirement. Large travel segments are poorly served or not served at all by the travel trade. There is a vast potential need for technological and service improvement.

References

1 Green H, Hunter C and Moore B. Assessing the environmental impact of tourism development. *Tourism Management* Vol 11, Number 2. June 1990. Butterworth-Heinemann pp 119-120

2 Downe M. International Travel in the 1990s. How is the industry shaping up? British Airways Business Life 22. August/September 1989. p 20

3 International Rail Services for the United Kingdom. British Railways Board. December 1989. p 8

5 Market product relationships in development

The product is the foundation of the marketing programme and the market is the basis for product development. The product/market fit table is the launch pad, in as much as it attempts to fit the right product to the right market and segment. Market analysis and a realistic assessment of market potential are key components of the development plan. Once the development has taken place marketing will be vital for its success, indeed a marketing strategy should be developed as part of the plan.

We have seen in earlier chapters how tourism has grown into an industry of international significance and how it is beginning to evolve. Increasingly the products and the services have to meet consumer expectations. Whether the development is demand led as in the case of the Costa Brava development, or supply led as in the case of Aviemore and Languedoc Roussillon, there must be a market and analysis of demand in the markets must be complemented by an analysis of tourist resources at the destination. *Demand led* product development responds to an existing demand such as a need for sun, sea and sand holidays by sun starved northerners. *Supply led* products or even destinations are developed and subsequently go in search of a market or markets.Tourism development must be market led.

In tourism there are three distinct markets: the domestic, the international, and the day visitor. While the internationally accepted definition of tourist (*see* Chapter 1) generally excludes the day visitor, the facility provider very often needs to take this market into account in his planning. A development may be designed to cater exclusively for the international traveller–Kenya, Mauritius, Bermuda, the Seychelles are all examples. But even where there is no local demand tourism generally works better if local people are involved from the outset.

The tourist product is a satisfying activity at a desired destination. Many independent suppliers–transporters, accommodation providers, facility operators, caterers and retailers–provide the tourist experience. Independent yet interdependent and it is for the official tourist board to supply the destination co-operative marketing base, the focal point for consultation as the basis for product development. The marketers can shape the development and present it in an attractive and appealing way.

Plans must look at the existing situation; analyse the strengths and weaknesses of the destination, the opportunities and the constraints to growth. This must be the foundation of the strategy and the strategy itself must be related to official tourism policy; the agreed policy and objectives for the destination whether country, region or resort. Objectives will be derived from an agreed mission statement and aims and could include such things as increased employment, increased foreign currency earnings, enhanced amenities for leisure and recreation, conservation. The mission statement should be succinct (usually not more than 30 words) and address three things: what do we do? how do we do it? and for whom do we do it? Aims further develop the purpose for which an organisation exists. Objectives are specified planned achievements for furthering aims and may be specified in terms of planned output or performance. Targets provide the quantified steps towards achieving objectives, usually within a specified timescale. Together they form a hierarchy with targets as a stepping stones to objectives – objectives a stepping stone to aims.Unless it is recognised that the market dictates though there will almost certainly be an undisciplined response by the producers. Planning attempts to rationalise and take the guesswork out of decision making but there must be creativity, a leap in the imagination, if developments are not to be sterile and they must be perceived to be special, to provide a quality and a consistency.

Philip Kotler defines marketing strategy as:

> a set of principles for adjusting the marketing programme to changing conditions. Marketing strategy acts as an overall plan that comprehends various possible developments and states the principles for meeting them.[1]

> If the development is sound new traffic movement will grow rapidly and may continue with reducing marketing investment for some years.[2]

All products though have a life cycle, which may be short or long. The product is launched, grows to maturity, plateaus, and then gradually declines. The decline can be halted and reversed however with refurbishment, representation or additional features. It can also be reversed with a change of branding and positioning or even a fresh injection of publicity. The hotel notching itself up a couple of stars following a refurbishment programme, the provision of en suite bathrooms, a health and leisure complex, is an obvious example of arresting and reversing product decline. Madame Tussaud's has had a long life cycle stretching back almost two hundred years but there is a constant injection of new models and new techniques into the show to sustain interest.

Strategies must take a long term view and targets should be set for regular monitoring and appraisal. Marketing tactics may well have to be changed in the light of experience but the overall long term strategy will remain in place.

SWOT analysis

The French, in their Languedoc Rousillon development, started within a blank sheet of paper, an undeveloped coastal area with little or no existing infrastructure. More usually though there is an existing infrastructure and the options for development may be limited or dependent on securing changes in the infrastructure. A good starting point is to undertake a SWOT analysis, identifying honestly the strengths and weaknesses, the opportunities and the threats or constraints. The analysis will almost certainly be based on the destination's strengths and weaknesses before undertaking further analysis into the particular development.

Table 5.1 Strengths and weaknesses analysis of London

Strengths	Weaknesses
Heritage appeals	
Entertainment, including theatre and the performing arts	Tickets touts Lack of nightlife
Tradition and pageantry Royalty	
Museums and galleries	Closed at certain times, e g Sunday mornings or Mondays
International airports (Heathrow, Gatwick, Stansted)	Airport delays
Shopping	Litter, restricted Sunday trading
Wide spectrum of accommodation	Perceived high cost, lack of budget accommodation
Wide spectrum of cuisine	Poor perception of food

Table 5.1 Strengths and weaknesses analysis of London

Strengths	Weaknesses
Varied attractions	Shortage of coach parking Many closed Sunday mornings
Business centre	Lack of national exhibition centre
English–main language of communication	
Private hospitals and clinics	Perceived high costs
High quality British goods/design	Perceived high costs
Good spread of markets	Marketing spend by BTA being spread too thinly

The developer as well as the marketer must be scrupulously objective in undertaking this analysis. The charting of resources is the beginning of the work on strategy and it should embrace perceptions as in the example above. Similarly new legislation can bring about changes such as Sunday trading in the example. Some attempt should be made at forecasting when Sunday trading legislation might be enacted. There are clues, usually in a political party's manifesto or the announced Government programme. The characteristics of the destination have a substantial influence on the marketing programmes and so on product development. The product in turn is the foundation of the marketing programme affecting communications strategy, choice of markets, positioning and so on. Product analysis is also the key to segmentation.

Market analysis and segmentation

A thorough analysis will point up the market potential and the potential offered by particular market segments. The marketer who undertakes this analysis will also be identifying the external factors which are impinging on his marketing, the operational environment in which the marketing of the product is to be orchestrated. The external factors such as economic growth rates, inflation, exchange rates, political stability, competition, consumer legislation/protectionism, constitute the forces which determine the marketing opportunities and constraints. Chapters 3 and 4 looked at markets and segments offering potential on an international basis.

Tourism marketing needs to be selective because no service, no tourism product, no destination can satisfy the wants and needs of the total market.

Market research will need to be undertaken to determine the size and worth of markets and segments. Measuring markets is an essential part of strategic and marketing planning. But planned developments are not so much concerned with market measurement as market potential, which involves forecasting techniques. This forecast of potential will help to guide the planners to make informed judgements within certain parameters. It will provide a range of options.

The OECD publishes an annual digest on trends, governments' policies and specific sector studies which provides valuable data for developments studies.

Destination/tourist organisations can very often be enormously helpful in providing data on individual markets and segments. Many NTOs produce strategic guidelines for the industry from which their own marketing strategies derive and these will almost certainly include forecasts for up to five years ahead for individual markets. It is always worthwhile consulting the researchers and statisticians of the national or regional tourist boards who will not only allow access to data held in their offices or libraries but will very often be able to suggest other useful sources. This is no substitute for undertaking specific research but it will narrow the range and almost certainly the cost of that research.

There must be a clearly identified market for any product. As far back as 1968 the Xerox Corporation in the USA produced a machine which could produce a long distance high speed facsimile of a document, but it is only in recent years that the fax has become so widely used. In the 1960s Xerox felt that there was insufficient demand for a machine with such a capability outside the USA and consequently did not add it to their product range.

A honeypot development can create a market for other products. For example the development in Manchester of GMex, an exhibition centre from a disused Victorial railway station brought a number of hotel developments in its wake – some created from redundant buildings. Similarly in Birmingham the National Exhibition Centre spawned hotel development: likewise the Conference Centre in Brighton. Alas, hotel developers too often wait too long and so pay a higher price. A case in point is London's Docklands where land values were very cheap but have increased substantially over the past ten years. Only now are we beginning to see hotel developments. Hotel developers were slow to spot the market potential even after the transport system was in place.

Strategic plans for developments are not so much concerned with market measurement as market potential which involves forecasting techniques. This forecast of potential will help to guide the planners to make informed judgements within certain parameters and will provide a range of options. See Appendix to this chapter on *Forecasting*.

Having analysed products, markets and segments as part of the diagnostic process of planning, the important next stage is to match the right product against the right market and the right segment within that market. For attractions, segments will include specific foreign markets, the domestic market and day visits; for an hotel, specific foreign markets and segments within those markets: coach tour groups, incentive groups, business travellers, etc; the domestic market: business and leisure travellers, the short break market, leisure learning, activity holidays; and the local market: banquets, weddings, club dinners, hobby groups etc. As an exercise it will help to establish the potential for the development but it will also be the launch pad for the marketing plan since marketing is concerned with communicating the right product to the right market and the right segment.

Table 5.2 Product/market fit table for hotel

	Local	Domestic			Overseas					
		Up to 100 miles	Up to 200 miles	Rest	A	B	C	D	E	F
Meetings/Hobby groups										
Weddings/Banquers										
Corporate lunches/dinners										
Association lunches/dinners										
Independent leisure										
Car touring leisure										
Leisure learning weekend										
Off peak break										
Coach touring										
Independent business										
Corporate meetings										
Trade fairs										
Incentive travel										

Branding

Attention will need to be given at an early stage to branding: the brand name and more particularly the brand image – the perceived quality and symbolic features of the product. Branding is essential to distinguish your product from someone else's. In time the brand will become a valuable asset as a combination of physical and symbolic features, rational and emotional elements which, if appealing, will be purchased and continued to be purchased. To survive though the brand must be *protected* by ensuring consistent quality and value. If the brand does not perform consistently the consumer will reject it. The brand name of a destination sometimes can be changed. While it is impossible to change the name of a country, a coastline can be branded as the Cote d'Azur, the Costa del Sol. A resort can be named to be almost a brand name, such as Surfers' Paradise in Queensland, which is central to the resort's personality. Branding too needs to be research based even though it is perhaps the most creative of marketing techniques.

> For the destination marketer, a successful branding strategy can act as a guarantee of quality for the tourist; it can provide leverage over middlemen such as agents and airlines; provide a means of controlling a destination's image; and give direction to operators, agents and other businesses in the preparation of promotional material thus obtaining consistency in the communication to the tourist.[3]

References

1 Kotler P 1967 *Marketing Management* Prentice Hall Inc. p 281.
2 Jefferson A, Lickorish L J *Marketing Tourism: A Practical Guide* Longman Group UK Ltd. p 185.
3 Cossens J J. Unpublished thesis submitted for Master's degree, University of Otago, Dunedin, New Zealand. November 1989. p 100.

Appendix Extract From Marketing Tourism – A Practical Guide 1989. Longman

Forecasting

Forecasting related to market measurement has a special and key function. It represents target setting, and is a principal objective of market planning. The individual market studies will be compared with the national and as appropriate regional studies. Projection of historic trends will be modified firstly, by reference to product changes and major supply developments, secondly, by taking into account external factors (national economic situation, international market situation, fiscal burdens, inflation and political stability).

Finally, the commercial operator, whether in the public or private sector will seek the maximise revenue and profits in moving towards maximum efficiency in use of resources. His own market measurement will have indicated changes in his market share, new opportunities, the competitive advantages or dangers. Since tourism is essentially a market force requiring a package of services and attractions, the individual operator must take into account his partners' forecasts and plans related to them, and in marketing seek to take advantage of the cooperative task where this supports his own competitive role, as in part it will.

Forecasting methods will follow the national pattern, but must be modified in the light of the specific service or trader's market study, and forward plan remembering that the forecast in this case is the business target or plan.

Measuring market potential

An essential aspect of market measurement relates to market potential. This involves forecasting techniques. Forecasting is not an exact science. Usually estimates of future traffic reflect potential not necessarily targets. The object is to guide, to assist informed judgements in marketing and development. It is not a 'crystal ball' exercise predicting the future but rather giving indications of possibilities, a range of options, orders of magnitude and not precise figures. Costs and benefits, favourable and unfavourable factors, strengths and weaknesses must be considered in assessing likely trends. Furthermore, in the exercise of options account must be taken of proposed action to exploit markets, to use the marketing forces to achieve certain objectives.

The principal methods of forecasting are:

(a) the projection by extrapolation of historic trends;
(b) extrapolation, subject to the application of `weights' or variables.

These may be accompanied by the Delphi method of structured group discussions by experts on changing trends and key factors determining future traffic flows. The `Delphi' discussion will be used primarily to evaluate weights and variables.

The third method is the use of mathematical models. While this was popular in the earlier periods of growth in mass tourism in the 1950s and 1960s the more sudden and dramatic changes in economic and social backgrounds, and the increasing strength and dynamism of market forces have made the models imprecise and too theoretical for use on their own. Market surveys, identifying trends from listening to the market place have become vital factors in estimations of potential.

In recent years the European Travel Commission has carried out forecasting exercises in cooperation with the principal tourism industry sectors. Methods involved projections, study of industry sector reports, and group discussions. The blend of specialist economic, market research and marketing knowledge and experience resulted in remarkably accurate medium-term forecasting (five to ten years), offering a range of possibilities on a high, medium and low basis. The studies have been repeated. Ideally the potential estimates need to be carried out on a rolling forward basis covering five to ten years, giving ranges of growth indicating the scenarios or likely external and market conditions. Clearly, the studies must take into account not only the longer term changing trends, traffic growth rates but basic `external' factors such as GNP and personal disposable income, likely tax and other fiscal changes, purchasing power, which might be affected by fluctuating exchange rates, political factors, unrest or restriction. For example, the introduction of visas for Americans and other non-EEC visitors as a security measure by the French had a bad effect on their transatlantic business in late 1986 and in 1987.

The Institute Transport Aerien in Paris carried out the first very detailed forecasting exercise for the European Travel Commission in 1980. Aviation and Tourism International completed a second monitoring exercise for the Commission in 1983. The following table from the latter report indicates the forecasts made, the timescale and looking back how forecasts compared with the results.

Comparison of 1990 forecasts

	ITA 'Middle'	ATI 'Most likely'
WORLD TOURIST ARRIVALS		
Annual growth	6.4% (1)	5.1% (2)
1990 forecast	536 M	415 M
ETC EUROPE ARRIVALS		
Annual growth	5.1% (3)	5.1% (2)
1990 forecast	242 M	239 M
MAIN OVERSEAS flOWS		
USA		
Annual growth	3.5% (3)	5.0% (2)
1990 forecast		
European arrivals	16.0 M	14.5 M
US departures	–	6.3 M
Canada		
Annual growth	4.0% (3)	4.0% (2)
1990 forecast		
European arrival	3.7 M	2.9 M
Canadian departures	–	1.1 M
Japan:		
Annual growth	7.6% (3)	6.7% (2)
1990 forecast		
European arrivals	4.1 M	3.0–3.3 M
Japanese departures	–	0.7–0.75 M

(1) From 1979 base (2) From 1982 base (3) From 1978 base

In the first case the economic recession, the oil crises and the end of a long period of continuous growth with slowly emerging changes in lifestyle and behaviour affected the forecasts. The severity of the recession and the speed and scale of other major trends were underestimated – not surprisingly. The second forecast by ATT usefully compared with the earlier forecasts has proved in the longer term remarkably accurate for world travel and for ETC Europe, although not so accurate for Europe, including the countries of eastern Europe.

Both studies were very thorough in their analysis of demand determinants including income elasticity, GDP, price changes and especially exchange rates relative to other competing goods and services. ATI used a `Delphi' type seminar to evaluate determinants and trends. Generally both groups of experts came to similar conclusions regarding the principal factors affecting future travel movements. This comparison of past studies not only vindicates the experts' work and their methods, but provides a valuable case history. Estimates of broad trends need to be on a longer term basis–five to ten years. They should cover a broad field; in this case Europe and the world. They should be seen as indications of potential, and variations from the anticipated trend expected. These changes need careful analysis as they will normally reflect important demand changes or market response to alteration in the key demand determinants. As these were clearly not expected there will be many lessons to be learnt by management and marketers. Variations represent major shifts in demand patterns, not simply changes in one geographic market or one segment, or in one destination area. This can happen for a number of reasons including marketing and price relativity. There is free and fierce competition and the tourist can switch patronage between competing areas while the total market increases.

The international forecasts are necessary checkpoints in national and regional market and development planning. The same principles should be used for national and regional strategies and plans.

Part II: Development strategies

Professor C L Jenkins

6 Tourism development strategies

The aim of this chapter is to consider the nature of, and the need for, development strategies for the tourism sector. The use of the plural, strategies is intentional. No two countries, or even areas within countries are likely to face identical problems at the same time. Strategies for development of tourism as with other sectors of economic activity, need to reflect not only current problems and concerns, but also future aspirations. There is, for example, considerable differences in approaching the formulation of a tourism development strategy in developed as opposed to developing countries. Strategy is used in the comprehensive sense to embrace both policy formulation and implementation.

In considering such a wide subject, it is preferable to concentrate on concepts and activities at macro or national level, although many of the concepts relating to policy formulations are equally relevant to regions or projects. The main focus is on the development of tourism locations be they at national, or sub-national level, and with prime emphasis given to international tourism development, noting the needs, opportunities and problems this form of business brings with it.

Formulating a policy for the tourism sector

Many of the world's countries now regard tourism as an important and integral aspect of their development strategies. In the literature on tourism, most studies give emphasis to the economic benefits derived from tourism. These benefits are usually encapsulated in contributions to foreign exchange earnings, government revenues, regional development stimuli, and creation of employment and income.

It is however, necessary to remember that tourism is more than an economic activity. It is, in essence, a massive interaction of people[1], demanding a wide range of services, facilities, and inputs which generate opportunities and challenges to host countries.

The multi-faceted nature of tourism does not permit it to be described as an *industry* in a technical sense; it has no single production characteristic or defined operational parameters. Its economic dimension cannot occur without inputs of a social, cultural and environmental nature.

It is this wide ranging and complex nature of tourism which requires careful analysis. Individual *ad hoc* responses to tourism opportunities and problems do not constitute a *policy for tourism*. Such responses might merely provide short-term solutions to essentially long-term problems.

There is no simple consensus on what is meant by the term policy. The Oxford Dictionary offers two definitions: 'prudent conduct' and 'a course of general plans of action'. What may be implied from both definitions is the notion of a reasoned consideration of alternative options. In tourism, with its many complexities and manifestations, it is often very difficult to define options let alone select a preferred course of action. Despite these difficulties, countries do require a policy or policy guidelines for the tourism sector. In this context we may pose two questions: why is such a policy necessary? and who should formulate the tourism policy?

Why do we need a tourism policy?

A large number of reasons may be offered to support the view that a country, particularly a developing country, should devise a policy for tourism. In addition to the basic argument that resources should be used and allocated as efficiently as possible, as an international export sector, tourism has made important contributions to many countries' economies. Tourism may also have other features which are of significance:

1. Tourism is often a substantial source of *hard* foreign exchange earnings.
2. As an export sector, tourism does not face trade or quota restrictions which confront many exports of manufactured goods, raw materials, and primary products.
3. Foreign and domestic tourists make use of a country's natural infrastructure eg climatic features, history, geography culture, etc. These attractions are *of the country* and are not specifically designed. In economic terms, tourism's use of the natural infrastructure has a low marginal cost.
4. Tourism is a relatively labour intensive activity; it has good potential for job creation, one of the major and continuing needs of the developing countries, and some developed countries.

5. As an amalgam of service and product demands, tourism can act as a catalyst for demand for goods from other sectors, e g foodstuffs, services, handicrafts, etc. In economic terms, there exist substantial linkage possibilities between tourism activity and other sectors in the economy. In many countries, there would be substantial demand for construction services arising from tourist's need for accommodation and infrastructure.

As demand for tourism increases, it will bring with it not only opportunities for linkages with other sectors in the economy, but also consequences of a social, cultural, and environmental nature. These consequences, eg overcrowding at airports, traffic density, noise, pollution, etc will affect both public and private sectors. In these areas where tourism impacts on the country and society, there may well be conflicts with competing demands from other sectors of the economy, or with community interests at large. An example would be where tourism development competes with agricultural interests for land, with the consequent increase in land prices making it difficult for nationals to own land. In Chiang Mai in Northern Thailand, prime agricultural land has been sold by local farmers at prices, for them, which are very high. The purchasers, many who reside in Bangkok, regard these prices as cheap compared to city and urban levels.

How can the interests of the community and society be considered, and if necessary, protected? Who balances economic gains from tourism against possible disbenefits relating to social, cultural and environmental values? There is no simple, single answer to these questions, but without a considered policy approach, there can be no logical determination of such issues. A current example from Scotland relates to the continuing debate to either further develop ski facilities in the Cairngorm mountain region or to prohibit further development to conserve and protect Britain's only alpine region. In many tropical countries, the World Bank has halted a large number of projects which although economically attractive, are now expected to generate some environmental damage. At a global level, concern about the *greenhouse* effect has transcended national considerations.

In developed countries there exist formal and informal consultation procedures and administrative systems which provide a structure to discuss and resolve such issues. A well developed and innovative private sector usually exists in these countries. Government is essentially seen as an enabling force to stimulate development, with entrepreneurial activity coming from the private sector.

In most developing countries, government has the central and dominant role in the planning process. This role might be adopted through political preference, or necessity, or both. No two countries are similar in the range and difficulty of problems they face. Many developing countries have weak, embryonic tourism sectors; other countries have vigorous, developed tourism sectors, and in the latter countries, much of the investment, management and development in tourism is from private sector initiative. However, as a general proposition, most developing countries are characterised by a scarcity of development resources. Tourism, as one sector of the economy, must compete for these scarce resources. The advocates of tourism must convince government that the sector is worthy of support.

In many countries, government has already accepted the importance of tourism, but few have given careful consideration to the type of tourism they want; to what extent their declared aims are realistic; and what needs to be done to achieve those aims. Such questions are at the heart of tourism policy formulation.

Role of government in tourism policy formulation

While there is considerable and continuing debate surrounding the role of government in the formulation of tourism policy, most observers would accept that some degree of intervention is essential.[2] In developing countries it can be argued that a greater degree of intervention by government is required to achieve material objectives because of the absence of a developed and innovative private sector. In many countries, eg India, Bangladesh, Jamaica, government has undertaken an entrepreneurial role to ensure that *pioneer* activities are initiated. For example, a government decision to invest in and manage hotels for tourists might represent a philosophical and political dimension to policy – or reflect a circumstance where private sector capital is not available for, or unwilling to invest in, tourist attractions and amenities.

The nature of government involvement in tourism might be usefully described as active or passive. Active involvement is characterised as a deliberate action by government introduced to favour the tourism sector. Passive involvement occurs when government undertakes an action which may have implications for tourism, but is not specifically intended to favour or influence tourism development. Some further refinement of these categories will emphasise the role that governments play in tourism development.

A *Passive involvement*

The characteristics of passive involvement by government in tourism might be categorised into mandatory and supportive actions.

Passive mandatory actions will usually be linked with legislation. Three examples will illustrate this concept.First, a government enacts legislation relating to the employment of foreign nationals within a country. Second, a government introduces legislation offering investment incentives. Third, government negotiates a bilateral air services agreement. In these examples, government is using its mandatory authority to introduce legislation which relates to the country as a whole and is not intended to discriminate in favour of the tourism sector, although these measures may have implications for tourism.

Supportive actions arise when government does not deliberately inhibit the development of the tourism sector, but neither does it actively encourage it. An example might be where government provides some general training courses, clerical, secretarial, languages, etc which may or may not have relevance to the needs of the tourist sector. Although these actions might support the needs of the tourism sector, it is not a provision specifically aimed at the sector.

B *Active involvement*

This implies not only a recognition by government of the specific needs of the tourism sector but also the necessity for its operational participation to attain stated objectives. It is this specific action which distinguishes active from passive involvement and it can be categorised as follows:-

Managerial – in this case government not only set tourism objectives (possibly in a Tourism Development Plan) but also introduce the necessary organisational and legislative support to attain the objectives. In terms of the three examples cited above, government can discriminate in favour of foreign nationals seeking employment in tourism rather than employment in other sectors. Secondly, government can introduce specific tourism investment incentives (and might establish a Tourism Development Bank), and thirdly, it could negotiate bilateral air agreements with the specific aim of fostering tourist traffic. In these circumstances, government involvement is selective and specific.

Developmental – in this case developmental involvement is seen where government or its agencies undertake an operational role in the tourist sector. This role might be adapted for ideological reasons, as in centrally planned economies. However, as noted above, in many regional countries governments have undertaken this role because of the inability or unwillingness of the private sector to become involved in tourism. The Indian Tourism Development Corporation (ITDC) was established to not only invest in tourism facilities and services, eg hotels, airlines, travel agencies, etc, but also to operate these services. At the time when the Corporation was introduced there was a lack of both investment funds for tourism development in certain locations and also little interest by Indian entrepreneurs to become involved in the development of the tourism sector The ITDC was seen as a means of not only developing tourism facilities to meet economic criteria, but also in a social sense to stimulate economic activity in regions where it was difficult to attract private capital.

The essence of active involvement by government in tourism is an action or series of actions which discriminate in favour of the tourism sector. It is pertinent to note that the nature and extent of this involvement will reflect not only the stage of development of a country, but also the prevailing political philosophy.

In socialist, centrally planned economies, the private sector is small or non existent and government assumes a dominant entrepreneurial role. In developed, mixed economy countries, most of the entrepreneurial investment has been made by the private sector with government providing infrastructure and other selective help. Whatever the political views of government, its involvement is likely to reflect the importance of tourism within the economy. However, it is pertinent to note that the bastions of centrally planned economies – the countries of Eastern Europe – have now opted for market driven development with governments setting development parameters.

Most developing countries are characterised by a scarcity of resources for development purposes, with private sectors which have little experience of tourism as an industry. Not all development countries fit this generalisation, with India, Maldives, Sri Lanka, The Bahamas, etc, having well developed private sector tourism interests. But in other countries, government has to adopt an entrepreneurial role to become the dynamo for tourism development and growth. In many such countries, government is the largest employer of labour, the major source of investment funds, and the guarantor for foreign loans. One recognises Bauer's critique that the centralisation of development initiative does not make it necessarily more efficient and effective: 'comprehensive planning does not augment resources, it only concentrates power'[3]. However, for many developing countries with few export options available to earn hard currency, the attractions of tourism are very real to many governments.

Many of the problems inhibiting economic progress in the developing countries are intensifying. Continuing deterioration in their terms of trade, tariff and quota restrictions, all serve to make progress difficult. Recent political instability in areas such as the Gulf, Indian-Pakistani confrontation in Kashmir, affect governments and tour operators alike. Tourists are easily diverted from destinations and where this occurs, eg the Philippines, it adds to existing economic pressures. It also jeopardises current investment and employment in the tourism sector. Tourism cannot be developed without incurring substantial costs and governments need to have clear policies for the sector before large investment is made.

Policy areas

It is not possible or desirable to consider in great detail all those areas which impinge on tourism policy making. What is required is an acceptance of the notion that tourism policy must include considerations of economic and non-economic factors, international and domestic tourism, and that without agreed aims and objectives, formal development planning is likely to be uncoordinated and unsatisfactory. Some of the more important areas involving policy decisions are discussed briefly below.

Public or private development of tourism?

In many developing countries the private sectors will not have the experience, resources, and possibly, inclination to invest in tourism (as noted above). In most South Asian countries[4], governments have taken an active role in the development of tourism. Given the conflicts which will arise from uncontrolled growth of tourism, it is essential that government becomes involved in the sector. There is a growing awareness that tourism is not simply an economic activity. More attention is being given to the impact of international tourism on the host community. The non-economic impacts of tourism, social, cultural and environmental are now being given a higher priority by policy makers and planners[5]. Even in developed countries it is recognised that there are social and environmental limits to growth – and specifically to certain types of tourism development, in particular locations. In the United Kingdom, for example, the introduction of National Parks and areas designated as being of *scientific importance* reflect the need for balance in the approach to development.

International or domestic tourism?

Most developing countries have fostered the international tourism market for reasons noted above. However, the potential for domestic tourism should not be ignored, and to do so would be to ignore the Manila Declaration on World Tourism. Domestic tourism has an important role to play in strengthening national identities and values. In India the strengthening of national identity through domestic tourism has long been an important feature of policy. The Australian Bi-Centenary Year and European Tourism Year are further examples of tourism being used to intensify national identities.

It should also be noted that there is a considerable amount of intra regional tourism in the developing world, e g South Asian region. This type of tourism will also generate foreign exchange earnings, and is less likely to cause social and cultural conflict between hosts and guests. If this type of tourism is to be encouraged, it will have different needs and implications from simply concentrating on western tourist markets.

Scale of tourism development

Most countries have sought, as a policy objective, to maximise the numbers of tourists arriving in the country. This objective has often brought with it considerable problems of an economic, social, cultural and environmental nature. A more controlled and lower level of arrivals is aimed at in some countries, eg Bhutan, Pacific islands. It is now fashionable to describe small-scale tourism as *alternative tourism*. Whether such an approach is desirable, feasible, and possible will again require detailed examination not only of governments' objectives but also of the many factors which constitute a tourist destination. The term alternative tourism is ambiguous, and therefore has many possible interpretations. It is now clearly related to the more recent concepts of *eco* or *green* tourism. What do the terms mean? What are the policy implications?

All these concepts have a basic similarity in that they are concerned with sustainable tourism development. This sustainable development puts emphasis on the careful use of current tourism assets to ensure future availability. One of the related issues is the concept of carrying capacity; to encourage a level of development which optimises economic, social and cultural benefits within an environmentally acceptable limit. It is not a difficult ideal to express, but is very difficult to achieve in relation to development planning. This holistic approach is likely to become more central in tourism planning, but particularly in the developing countries, it has often to confront political realities.

In Indonesia, the main tourism destination is the island of Bali: 60 per cent of all visitors visit the island. Environmental and infrastructural limitations are becoming more apparent. Indonesia government policy is to use Bali as a distribution point to encourage visitors to travel to other islands – the marketing slogan 'Bali and Beyond' encapsulates the policy. In practice, the Government cannot introduce artificial measures to prevent tourists from visiting Bali because of the economic losses which would result. Although the Government is sensitive to the overuse and overdevelopment in Bali, economic determinants suggest a gradualist rather than revolutionary change. The scale of tourism development is dictated by market demand, and needs for controls are usually seen as being reactive rather than pro-active.

Integrated or enclave tourism?

Enclave tourism implies a conscious decision to segregate tourists from the general population. This form of development aims to attain the benefit of foreign exchange without the overwhelming of indigenous cultures by foreign tourists. In the 1960s Tanzania favoured enclave tourism developments to *protect* African culture from overwhelming contact with foreign tourists. At the resort level, Butlins Holiday Camps in the UK, Club Mediterranean in many countries of the world, and the Costa Smeralda development created by the Agha Khan, are different types of enclaves. These types of developments might be encouraged for reasons of cultural protection, security, social exclusiveness or sometimes to contain environmental impacts. There are many questions to be asked about this type of development before initiating construction.

There are different types of enclave developments which tend to feature more in developing countries where the gaps in income between visitors and hosts is greatest, and where cultural and social distinctiveness is most threatened.

It is apparent that the notion of tourism policy must embrace the wide differences between developed and developing countries and the significant variations between countries within those categories. Where tourism is seen as having a contribution to make to economic development there is an a *priori* assumption that resources should be used efficiently and effectively. In many countries there is a formal national planning process, with many governments having established ministries, agencies or planning departments. This national attention to planning focuses on the need to allocate scarce resources on a rational, prioritised basis. The allocation of resources needs to be seen against expected returns from investment in various sectors; the *weighting* of expected returns becomes an important point in the allocative process. For reasons suggested above, tourism is seen by many governments as a means of making a positive economic contribution to development – but the main question arising is how does a country optimise that contribution?

The optimisation of tourism's potential contribution is clearly linked to the need to

1. Develop objectives for the tourism sector, and
2. Formulate a policy to implement those objectives.

Both these stages of policy making involves government intervention. This does not mean that the private sector is not involved in policy discussions, but rather that national objectives should prevail over group, company or sector objectives. It is not unusual to see major differences in interest, approach and motivation for tourism investment between public and private sector agents. The need for tourism planning is to minimise these potential conflicts and to delineate a development framework within which the private sector might operate. It is suggested here that without governments' involvement in tourism planning, development of the industry will lack cohesion, direction, and short-term initiatives might well jeopardise longer-term potential.

Tourism development objectives

They should be specific; and are usually expressed in very broad and general terms. Without carefully considered objectives there can be no rational policy: if a policy is to be the means of attaining the objectives. Many countries have general objectives, eg to maximise the benefits from tourism, but little evident thought has been given to the way in which such an objective might be realised. Where even broad objectives have not been formulated, then the tourism sector will inevitably *drift* and can bring problems which might have been avoided.

In the developed countries there is also a need for a tourism policy. Government must set out the parameters within which it wants to see tourism develop. It should guide the private sector by clearly indicating what type and volume of tourism is acceptable, and in which locations. Government should interact with levels of local government to encourage tourism in specific regions. The successful development of tourism in cities like Glasgow, Bradford, and Manchester, demonstrate what can be achieved through local enterprise and initiative.

It must be recognised that even specific objectives might be unattainable, for an international tourism sector is essentially a dependent sector – that is, in the absence of a unique attraction, tourism demand is largely exogenously determined. This characteristic of international tourism demand is important because it requires each tourist-receiving country to realistically appraise it's tourism attractions not in terms of domestic but rather international competition. In a region, eg, the Caribbean with many countries offering very similar tourist attractions, intraregional and international competition will be great.

In refining broad tourism objectives to formulate a policy there are a number of basic stages which should be examined and their interrelationship explored.

A *Evaluation of tourism supply*

As noted above, many countries have attractions of touristic merit. The important question is whether that country has a comparative advantage in its particular attractions. This notion of comparative advantage is essentially international. Domestic tourism is an important means of *topping* up demand in many countries. Any country attempting to break into the international tourism market, or committing further resources to the sector should carefully examine the availability, quality and price competitiveness of its tourism amenities. This evaluation is often best done by outside professionals if only to bring a degree of objectivity to the process. Such a process would identify the major and subsidiary tourism attractions, rank them against regional and other competition to give some indication of the market segment which might be interested in, and attracted to such a country. A realistic evaluation of tourism supply will include not only current assets but also those with development potential. Such an evaluation of supply factors can then be related to an analysis of international tourism demand to facilitate a product market fit.

B *Analysis of tourism demand*

This will include the existing and potential market. In countries with large, established tourism sectors, the analysis will be related to ways in which demand can be increased and possibly diversified. Such considerations are often loosely described as the *marketing* of tourism. But perhaps tourism marketing and related promotional activities should be regarded as the natural consequence of an analysis of demand. This is an important point. Many countries can and do engage professional marketing consultants who provide a high level of service and expertise. A fundamental question to be asked is whether this expertise is provided within determined policy parameters – will it contribute to the overall objectives of the tourism sector? Unless objectives are determined in advance of marketing initiatives, these might contradict implied but not explicit objectives.

A rigorous analysis of demand will indicate certain growth parameters. These parameters will be guides to future development options which can be related to supply conditions and constraints. A careful analysis of supply and demand provides the information for the third major stage in the planning framework – the determination of tourism growth targets.

C Tourism sector growth targets

Targets should be based on a series of development options or scenarios as they are sometimes described. They should be more than an exercise in demand forecasting. These options should embrace three basic questions:

1. How many tourists can be attracted (Maximisation option).
2. How many tourists are wanted by season and region? When? Where? (Optimisation option)
3. What are the costs: economic, social, financial, and environmental, of supporting the desired level of tourists?

In practice, most countries concentrate on the first option. This is understandable because there are very serious problems related to the quantification of the second two options. This does not imply that to maximise tourist arrivals is necessarily efficient or cost-effective – 'big is not always beautiful!'

There are good reasons for believing that some of the smaller countries do not want large scale tourist sectors. In the Republic of The Seychelles the government has imposed a limit of 4,000 beds on the industry. This limit will help to avoid over-rapid growth, ease manpower shortages, and help to maintain the country as an up-market destination. The Himalayan kingdom of Bhutan has imposed a control on tourist arrivals through visas and strictly defined quotas. In both cases these small countries are very concerned with the problems associated with rapid increases in tourist arrivals. They must therefore give careful consideration to the staged growth of the tourism industry and devise means to control the rate and type of expansion. In essence, this approach relates the tourism target to national objectives which in turn require government involvement and concern. To eschew involvement weakens any planned growth strategy and allow private sector interests to expand at the pace and in the type of tourism it wants. In these circumstances, tourism grows as a simple reaction to market forces. In other circumstances, market forces may be stultified by the absence of government guidelines and support for the tourism sector. In the 1980s tourism development in the Solomon Islands was prevented by the very complex system of land ownership which made it very difficult for potential foreign investors to attain good title to land. It was not until the government intervened to facilitate the leasing of land together with protection for communal landowners' rights, that development could proceed.

It should be noted that for many countries their type of tourism is determined by forces outside their control. Distance from main generating countries, transport links, costs and prices, *image*, all contribute to the overall competitiveness of a destination. The visitor flows are also affected by the information and advice provided by the tour-operator and travel agents in the tourist-generating country.

For various reasons, once a country has determined its growth target, it then has to consider the implications of this target in relation to existing tourism sector components.

D Tourism sector components

Although the components of the tourism sector – accommodation, transport, services – are common to all destinations, these characteristics will vary between countries in terms of volume, value and quantity. Variations will depend on a range of factors – stage of development of the tourism sector, historical precedent, local circumstances, etc. Some governments will have a higher degree of involvement in tourism than others. Whatever the particular circumstances of a country might be, the adoption of a tourism growth target will have implications for component activities which must be considered. Such consideration reinforces the interdependence of tourism as an activity and demands an integrated approach to policy formulation. Below, some of these component activities are briefly reviewed:-

1. Tourism Investment – Does the tourism growth target require new investment in the sector, or should it better utilise existing capacity? If new investment is required, who will finance it and on what terms? Should foreign investment be encouraged and if so, should investment incentives be offered and at what level?[6] Most developing countries have actively sought foreign investment and

are likely to do so in the future.[7] The questions of the type and level of incentives offered are very important but poorly researched aspects of tourism investment.

2. Manpower Planning and Training – Any future development of the tourism sector must involve consideration and analysis of the present and future manpower and related training requirements of the tourism industry. Careful analysis is needed to ensure that training targets are realistic – to overtrain in terms of numbers of trainees and the level of training offered, is wasteful of resources. Many *tourism training institutes* are related to the training of workers for the hotel and restaurant subsector. The tourism sector is much wider and includes travel agency staff, national tourism office staff, tour guides, information officers, etc.

In many ways the quality of a country's tourism personnel determine the visitor's image of that country. Irrespective of the degree of refinement attained in tourism planning, it is at the level of personal contact that the most effective form of tourism monitoring can take place. The need for manpower planning again indicates the integrated nature of planning for tourism – without proper demand studies, much of the training offered might be irrelevant and wasteful if there are no employment opportunities. Where vocational training is proposed, there should be sound reasons for it being implemented and it should be cost-effective.

3. Accommodation Sub-Sector – The main concern here is to what extent does a tourism growth target affect the existing accommodation sub-sector. Will increased demand, raise existing occupancy levels – or will it divert the market? Does the growth target require a change in the quality of accommodation offered? What is the time-lag for bringing new units on stream? It can be argued that education and training in themselves are beneficial. However, vocational training which includes tourism is usually job related and therefore a specific rather than a general provision.

In the short-term 2–3 years, it might be very difficult to increase the accommodation stock. The development margin will depend very much on local construction industry capabilities and availability of equipment. The latter factor is likely to be a major constraint where a tourism project is of a scale very much larger than those previously built. Another factor could arise if a country attempts to change it's tourism image, perhaps by trying to move up-market to attracting quality tourists. In this way, the scale and type of facilities to be developed will obviously have implications for the level of investment required.

4. Land Use Policy – An important constraint on the rate of development of tourism in some countries is the availability and

ownership of land. Land use planning is of considerable importance to tourism development; as is the question of land ownership. There may also be social considerations, for concentrated tourism developments usually have the effect of raising land prices and might create a tourist enclave or ghetto.[8] Land ownership and particularly foreign participation in land acquisition, are emotive as well as economic issues and must be carefully considered in any tourism development strategy. In some ways, barriers existing to foreign ownership, and on leasing of land, constitute a constraint on the over-rapid growth of tourism.

5. Transport Policies – There are two main points to be considered here – the movement of tourists to the country and the distribution of tourists within the country. Many developing countries' airlines have established enviable levels of service and reputation. Many countries have pioneered innovative fares; become involved in tourism promotion; and instituted attractive *stop-over* options. Most carriers realise the importance of tourism and tourists for their survival and a number of airlines have made impressive efforts to attract these travellers.

Where tourism is important to a country, transport policy both external and domestic, is a vital aspect of tourism development. The Indian Railway's introduction of the *Palace on Wheels* is a very interesting aspect of a development aimed at the international tourism market. Although tourist demand is of very little significance to the Indian Railway system, it is a very unusual contribution to overall Indian tourism.

However, in both developed and developing countries, there is often a very weak linkage between policies for transport and policies for tourism. The two areas are interdependent. In the UK the tourism possibilities arising from the Channel Tunnel would have been enhanced by the Government finding a high-speed link from the Tunnel to London. The often conflicting development aims of airlines and tourism sectors is a continuing weaknesses in many countries and continues to limit the benefits that tourism can generate.

The above five components of tourism planning are presented to illustrate the need for a comprehensive view of tourism and of its development. The component list is not exhaustive – it did not include a discussion of the potential for intersectorial linkages and the possible measures that governments might use to encourage these linkages, and minimise the need for imports. These, and the many other considerations arising from tourism development, cannot be detailed here, but their mention further emphasises the need for an overview to be taken of tourism and its social and economic effects on a country.

Monitoring tourism

From the above comments it is apparent that tourism is an activity of wide dimensions involving many organisations in both the public and private sectors, both domestic and abroad. This complexity makes it a difficult sector to manage and control. To monitor the sector's growth and development will require a national organisation with the responsibility and authority to undertake this task. Monitoring implies the tracing of developments against objectives and performance indicators. In economic and environmental areas, measurement techniques are well established. In relation to the social and cultural impacts of tourism, changes are often noticed over a long period of years, and are difficult to monitor in a quantitative way.

One of the great problem areas of tourism relates to its alleged social effects on resident populations. Governments must be aware of these problems and attempt to *manage* them by finding appropriate solutions. It is impossible at this general level to suggest *solutions*. It is, however, essential that the problems of tourism are not ignored, for they are unlikely to go away and many fundamentally effect the visitor–host relationship as well as country image. Because of this social dimension, government must be involved in the monitoring role because ultimately it will be responsible for the social consequences of tourism, particularly where they manifest themselves in political protest.

Evaluating tourism

The monitoring process feeds into the evaluatory exercise. The evaluation of the tourism sector should include a comprehensive review of the performance of the sector against established targets; an examination of component activity and consideration of future needs and changes. It might be argued that this evaluation is already done by national planners. In some countries it is attempted but often with inadequate data and with limited attention to the non economic dimension. More economic analysis of tourism would certainly improve the evaluatory process by providing sound quantitative data. At present, as noted above, much of this evaluation is made on subjective rather than on economic criteria.

Tourism is a complex activity: multisectoral in scope – with wide ramifications. In developing countries the limited technical and financial resources restrict analysis of tourism and its impact. In some countries expansion of visitor arrivals is the main priority with the implications of that priority not considered or debated. In other countries, tourism planning and tourism promotion are interchangeable terms, with promotion carried out without proper demand studies. For a tourism policy to be workable it must be relevant to the political and administrative structure of the host country and be capable of execution within the existing level of development and available resources of the country.

A tourism development strategy therefore promotes consideration of development objectives; the refinement of these objectives into policy statements; and the implementation of policy through development plans. Because of the interface between the public and private sectors, there is a role for government in this process. Many aspects of policy formulation cannot take place without government involvement. This does not imply that government has to be the dominant partner in the development process – it may prefer an enabling rather than operational role. Whatever role it adopts, it will certainly be seen as the arbiter between economic, social and environmental issues, which are likely to become more important. A strategy for tourism development not only focuses on the needs of the tourist and tourism sector but also on the host community without whose goodwill and receptiveness tourism cannot flourish.

References

1 Manila Declaration on World Tourism, Declaration A, Manila, October 1980, paras 7, 8, 14.
2 The Framework of the State's Responsibility for the Management of Tourism. W.T.O., Madrid.
3 Bauer P T *Dissent on Development:* Studies and Debates in Development, Economics, Harvard University Press, p. 72.
4 Ritcher L K *The Politics of Tourism in Asia*, 1989. University of Hawaii Press, Honolulu.
5 Murphy P '*Tourism - A Community Approach*', Methuen, 1985.
6 C L Jenkins The Use of Investment Incentives for Tourism Projects in Developing Countries. *Tourism Management* June 1982
7 S N Chib Financing Tourism Development - A Recipient's View. *International Journal of Tourism Management*, Vol. 1, No. 4, 1980.
8 E Rodenburg The Effects of Scale on Economic Development:: Tourism in Bali. *Annals of Tourism Research VII* (2) 1980.

7 Tourism and development

In Chapter 6 reasons were given for governments' encouraging tourism, and particularly international tourism, because of its contribution to development. In this Chapter, more detailed reasoning is given to support the case for tourism as a development initiative, but with consideration also being given to some of the problems associated with tourism. In Chapter 8, the impacts of tourism are considered.

Historically, tourism has been, and largely remains a by-product of developed and relatively affluent societies. In 1990, approximately 80 per cent of international tourist arrivals were in the developed regions of Western Europe and North America; this percentage has only marginally diminished over the past 40 years. Although predominantly an activity of developed countries, more tourists from these countries are now travelling to developing countries, and within the developing countries there are some significant movements of outward-bound tourists. The newly industrialised countries of Hong Kong, Taiwan and South Korea are increasingly contributing to international tourist arrival figures, and above all other examples, Japan has become an important generator of international tourists over the last decade. In these Asian countries, as economic development has improved, it has released more discretionary income to purchase foreign travel and holidays amongst other consumption possibilities. This increasing level of discretionary income is generating a class of leisure travellers in addition to the existing, and important, business travel market.

It is the dramatic impact of tourism in the developed world which has improved, and often provided the necessary example, for developing countries to follow. With tourism now a major international economic activity, and with the World Tourism Organisation (WTO) expecting it to become the major activity by the year 2,000, tourism obviously has advantages as a contributor to economic development which other activities might not have. What is important is the concept of comparative advantage; does the concentration of investment and resources into tourism generate more net economic benefit than if similar amounts of resources had been invested elsewhere, eg in agriculture or industry? The evaluation is, of course, complex and is outside the scope of this chapter. However, the issue is important because resources are scarce and need to be allocated amongst competing demands. Tourism has no prior claim for advantageous treatment, but should be regarded as one sector of an economy competing for available resources with others. Despite this caution, tourism has, particularly in developing countries, received substantial and continuing support from governments. Why should this have happened?

There are perhaps 7 main reasons why governments have supported tourism as part of their development strategies:

i) Historically, international tourism is a growth sector in the world economy. In the period 1979-1988 Table 7.1 indicates the comparatively good performance of international tourism arrivals and receipts compared to export performance generally.

Table 7.1 Average annual rate of increase of international tourist arrivals worldwide and by region 1979–1988

World – Regions	Average annual rate of increase		
	Arrivals	Receipts	Exports
World	4.0	9.8	6.2
Africa	7.9	11.6	–2.2
Americas	3.8	8.7	5.7
East Asia and The Pacific	11.1	16.7	10.1
Europe	3.0	9.1	6.7
Middle East	6.4	9.9	–5.4
South Asia	3.4	11.0	11.8

1 Asia and Oceania
2 Including South-East Asia
Source: WTO Current Travel and Tourism Indicators, Madrid, August 1989,

Over a longer period Table 7.2 shows the trends relating to international arrivals and receipts.

As a contributor to earnings from trade in services, Table 7.3 shows the strong impact that international travel receipts has had, particularly in some of the developing regions of the world.

Table 7.2 – Annual increase of arrivals of tourists from abroad, 1950 –88

Years	Arrivals (thousands)	Average annual increase/ change over previous year (%)
1950–1960	25,282–69,296	10.6
1960–1970	69,296–159,690	8.7
1970–1980	159,690–284,841	5.6
1981	288,849	1.4
1982	286,780	-0.7
1983	284,433	-0.8
1984	311,167	9.4
1985	325,725	4.7
1986	332,924	2.2
1987	358,659	7.7
1988 (re)	389,004	8.5

Source: World Tourism Organization (WTO)
Current Travel and Tourism Indicators, op cit, Section 5: Table 1, p 279

In 1988 receipts from international tourism accounted for approximately 7 per cent of world trade in goods and services. Tourism now ranks with oil and motor vehicles as one of the 3 main components of world trade. However, caution should always be used in interpretating international tourism statistics. Variation in collection methods, processing of data and use of definitions are a continuing problem. Most observers of international tourism would perhaps advocate that if anything, under-estimates of visitor arrivals and expenditure are made. For example, the above tables exclude earnings from international fare payments.

ii) Tourism is a major generator of hard currency earnings. The reason is that most tourists come from the developed countries of the world which invariably have *hard* that is, readily convertible currencies. Table 7.4 lists the world's top spenders on international tourism in 1988.

For developing countries, earnings of hard currency is particularly important as it is these earnings which permit the countries to buy the international goods and services which are needed to facilitate economic development. In most developing countries it is the acute scarcity of foreign exchange which frustrates the development effort. It is important to note that in countries such as India and Thailand, tourism is now the main source of foreign exchange earnings. In some respects, earnings from tourism are less subject to the regulations and limitations which usually surround international trade in goods and commodities.

Table 7.3 International travel receipts and trade in services 1980 and 1987

Regions	*Percentage share of travel receipts in service trade*	
	1980	1987
World	14.96	18.24
Developed market economy countries	13.29	16.07
Developing countries and territories	24.44	31.81
Socialist countries: Eastern Europe	23.13	24.22
Socialist countries: Asia	14.71	37.45
Developed market economy countries:		
Northern America 1/	9.59	10.09
Europe	15.22	19.51
EEC	13.71	18.29
EFTA	24.58	25.16
Other Europe 2/	23.57	38.78
South Africa	17.53	21.53
Asia 3/	4.36	5.97
Oceania 4/	20.06	34.44
Developing countries and territories:		
America	32.50	35.27
LAIA	38.48	35.54
Andean Group	16.41	24.02
CACM	35.90	32.79
CARICOM	47.91	82.28
Other America	9.65	14.58
Africa	19.29	33.20
North Africa	26.96	40.22
UDEAC 9.87	9.87	7.56
ECOWAS	8.02	19.99
CEPGL	13.59	8.68
Other Africa	16.45	30.59
Asia	18.98	29.36
West Asia	13.26	20.00
South and South East Asia	21.57	33.81
ASEAN	22.71	31.23
Bangkok Agreement	16.52	29.02
Other South and South East Asia	27.81	50.14
Oceania	28.44	20.91
Europe 5/	49.70	70.08
Socialists countries:		
Eastern Europe	23.13	24.22
Asia 6/	14.71	37.45
ACP	23.03	42.44

Source: WTO and IMF (Publications). Countries are presented on the basis of the UNCTAD grouping.

Notes: 1/ Canada and United States; 2/ Yugoslavia; 3/ Israel and Japan; 4/ Australia and New Zealand; 5/ Malta; 6/ China

W.T.O: Tourism Development Report, 1st Edition, 1988

Table 7.3 International travel receipts and trade in services (Cont.)

Abbreviations	
Developed market economy countries:	
EEC	**European Economic Community**: Belgium-Luxembourg, Denmark, France, Germany (Federal Republic of). Greece, Ireland, Italy, Netherlands, Portugal, Spain, United Kingdom.
EFTA	**European Free Trade Association**: Austria, finland, Iceland, Norway, Sweden, Switzerland.
	Other Europe: Faeroe Islands, Gibraltar, Liechtenstein, Monaco, Yugoslavia.
Developing countries and territories	
America	
LAIA	**Latin America Integration Association**: Argentina, Brazil, Chile, Mexico, Paraguay, Uruguay.
	Andean Group: Bolivia, Colombia, Ecuador, Peru, Venezuela.
CACM	**Central American Common Market:** Costa Rica, El Salvador, Guatemala, Honduras, Nicaragua.
CARICOM	**Caribbean Community**: Antigua and Barbuda, Bahamas, Barbados, Belize, Dominica, Grenada, Guyana, Jamaica, Montserrat, St. Christopher and Nevis, Saint Lucia, Saint Vincent and the Grenadines, Trinidad and Tobago.
	Other Americas: Bermuda, Cuba, Dominican Republic, Falkland Islands (Malvinas), French Guiana, Greenland, Guadeloupe, Haiti, Martinique, Netherlands Antilles, Panama, Suriname, U.S. Virgin Islands.
Africa	
	North Africa: Algeria, Egypt, Libyan Arab Jamahiriya, Morocco, Sudan, Tunisia.
UDEAC	**Customs and Economic Union of Central Africa**: Cameroon, Central African Republic, Chad, Congo, Equatorial Guinea, Gabon.
ECOWAS	**Economic Community of West African States**: Benin, Burkina Faso, Cape Verde, Cote d'Ivoire, Gambia, Ghana, Guinea, Guinea-Bissau, Liberia, Mali, Mauritania, Niger, Nigeria, Senegal, Sierra Leone, Togo.
CEPGL	**Economic Community of the Great Lakes Countries**: Burundi, Rwanda, Zaire.
	Other Africa: Angola, Botswana, Comoros, Djibouti, Ethiopia, Kenya, Lesotho, Madagascar, Malawi, Mauritius, Mozambique, Reunion, Sao Tome and Principe, Seychelles, Somalia, Swaziland, Uganda, United Republic of Tanzania, Zambia, Zimbabwe.

iii) Most individual countries and trade groups, eg European Economic Community (EEC), will seek to protect their domestic trade interests by imposing limitations on the amounts of certain imports allowed into the country in a period of time (quotas) or will impose variable levels of duty on imports (tariffs). Although these are limitations on world trade generally, they can provide specific obstacles for developing countries which have a narrow range of export opportunities. The ability of developing countries to increase economic growth through export-led initiatives will be artificially constrained. The competitive advantage for tourism as an export, is that the tourist travels to the destination and consumes the *holiday product* in situ providing opportunities for adding value to the services provided in the destination country.

Table 7.4 World's top spenders on international tourism in 1988

Country	International Tourism Expenditure (Million US$) 1988	Rank 1988
Germany (FR)	24 938	1
United States	23 092	2
Japan	18 682	3
United Kingdom	14 555	4
France	9 677	5
Netherlands	6 717	6
Canada	6 316	7
Italy	6 053	8
Switzerland	5 019	9
Austria	4 829	10
Sweden	4 570	11
Norway	3 405	12
Belgium	3 386	13
Mexico	3 205	14
Denmark	3 087	15
Australia	2 943	16
Spain	2 440	17
Kuwait	2 358	18
Finland	1 651	19
Malaysia	1 324	20
Brazil	1 249(1)	21
Korea (Republic of)	1 754	22
Israel	1 130	23
New Zealand	1 078	24

Note: Countries with international tourism expenditures of US$ 1 billion or more in 1988
1 1987
Source: WTO: Current Tourism and Trade Indicators, op. cit, Table 5, P 275

A further factor is that governments in developed countries are now unlikely for political and social reasons to impose limitations on citizens' rights to travel overseas, to where they wish to travel, and on how much they wish to spend. As such, these factors constitute an export opportunity free of the usual trade limitations. This does not lessen the international competition for tourists and tourists' expenditure, but it does remove regulatory barriers to entry to the market place.

iv) As noted above, as international tourists travel to the destination country, opportunities are created in these countries to use tourism as a catalyst for development. Tourism is an amalgamation of goods and services which constitute the holiday experience. The creation of employment and income will induce a multipler effect which can enhance these benefits to the country. These impacts will be examined in Chapter 8.

It should be mentioned that the impacts of tourism are important to both developed and developing countries.

In the United Kingdom tourism is the third main earner of foreign exchange, is estimated to provide over 2.5 million jobs, and is of particular regional significance in areas such as Scotland, Wales, Devon and Cornwall, etc. In many European countries such as France, Italy, Switzerland and Greece it is also a very important activity.

For the developing countries, in addition to hard currency earnings, tourism creates a need for services. Most developing countries have high rates of population growth, high levels of unemployment and under-employment, and a desperate need to find jobs for a growing labour force. Tourism is often seen as a labour intensive activity which provides more employment opportunities per unit of investment than other sectors of the economy. The arguments relating to the relative labour-intensity of tourism compared to other activities are often difficult to quantify. However, there is little doubt that in these countries tourism often provides a rapid means of employing low-skilled people. Again the benefits of this type of employment consideration must be given to longer-term development objectives and social as well as economic considerations.

Despite these problems many developed and under-developed countries see advantages in encouraging the growth of tourism to create employment opportunities often for low-skilled workers, and to generate linkage effects through the demand for associated services.

v) One of the factors which can increase the labour intensity of tourism, particularly in developing countries is the ability to develop tourism in such a way as to take advantage of resource-substitution possibilities.

In these countries where labour is not scarce and is therefore usually cheap, labour is substituted for capital. Some examples will demonstrate the point. In many developed countries hotels provide guests with tea-making facilities in their rooms, and may offer minimal porterage services; shoe-cleaning facilities if offered, are usually provided by a machine; entrance doors are usually triggered as guests approach by underfoot mechanisms. In these examples, labour which is expensive, is substituted by capital investment. In developing countries where labour is plentiful and cheap, people provide room service, porterage, and door attendance; the need for capital investment is avoided and more jobs are created.

There are limits to substitution possibilities, but opportunities are available to meet specific country needs. One of the attractions of tourism as a service industry is that labour intensity creates a level of personal service which is not usually available in developed countries, except in the highest quality hotels.

vi) Tourism makes use of natural infrastructure. Much of the tourism attraction of a country may focus on its climate, environment and scenery. In this way, economic value can be derived from resources which might have limited or no alternative use. If tourists are prepared to pay to use beaches, to visit national scenery, or to treck or climb mountains, then an economic value is being obtained from otherwise limited resources. An example is the income received by the Government of Pakistan from climbers who pay to climb certain mountains. Diving off the islands of Mauritius, Seychelles and in Micronesia are all examples of tourists generating income – and employment – from using these naturally available facilities. These examples have not included the historical and cultural resources which present generations have inherited from the past, eg temples, cathedrals, which tourists also visit.

vii) For many countries, tourism is viewed as a long-term development objective. As noted in Table 7.2, there is good empirical data to encourage the view that tourism appears to be resistant to major fluctuations in the world economy. Dislocating events tend to be regionalised, eg reduction in tourist arrivals in Europe in 1986 from the United States as a consequence of the Libya-United States dispute. The present crisis in the Gulf region will have a depressing impact on international tourist arrivals to that region and on neighbouring countries, eg Turkey, Egypt. Despite these problems, the main factors underlying the demand for international travel are strengthening.

First, in the main generating countries disposable incomes are increasing and more is being spent on international travel. Second, international travel, particularly by air, is becoming relatively cheaper. Third, more people view holidays as a normal expectation in their life-styles and evidence exists to support the view that holiday expenditure is protected above other consumer expenditure. Fourth, barriers to international travel are being reduced, with many governments and inter-government organisations making efforts to facilitate this movement.

The above reasons combine to provide a powerful argument for tourism being seen as a major force in the economic development spectrum. In particular, it has considerable advantages for developing countries and this was recognised as long ago as 1972 by Robert Erbes in his comment 'Everything seems to suggest that developing countries look upon tourism consumption as manna from heaven that can provide a solution to all their foreign settlement difficulties'[1]. In reality, tourism is neither a panacea or plague for development. It has to be carefully evaluated as a development option both domestically and internationally. Some of the main problems associated with tourism can be summarized as follows:

i) Despite the strong growth record of international tourism, growth trends are not applicable to every country or region. Acts of terrorism or even natural disasters can ruin a tourism season. Proximity to an incident is sufficient to cause dislocation. This problem is intensified when investment in tourism facilities cannot be utilised for other purposes, at least in the short term. For example, the political upheaval and violence which accompanied the last Jamaican election was sufficient to cause very bad publicity and a major decline in visitor arrivals. Fortunately, there is also evidence to suggest that tourists can be reassured about their safety and the industry can endure despite successive and sometimes continuous difficulties, eg Israel, South Africa, Northern Ireland.

ii) Although the tourist industry is an earner of hard currency, much of this can *leak* out of the economy, particularly in the developing countries. The need to attract foreign investment and consequent debt repayment can impose serious long-term problems for countries which are injudicious borrowers. Unless strong policies are adopted, much of the benefits of investment in tourism will not be received in the country but accrue to foreign interests.

iii) Tourism can be used as a development tool, and the opportunities to use its labour intensity is advantageous to many countries. The associated problem is to develop, educate and train the workforce to assume senior management position in the future. Many countries have failed to do this and blame the nature of tourism for this situation. As one Caribbean prime-minister once said 'tourism is turning our people into a nation of barkeepers and waiters'. There was truth in the statement. What was left unsaid was the failure of the government to develop policies to ensure that a stream of well-qualified people was available to train for these senior positions.

iv) Much of the infrastructure in tourism is highly specific. Although roads, water and sewerage systems can be used by non-tourists, if tourists stay away for whatever reason, much of the

foreign exchange earnings potential of the investment is frustrated, although debt servicing must continue.
v) Tourism is a very competitive activity with few countries having unique attractions. The possibility of destination-substitution is available to tour operators and tourists. In the long-haul market where the air fare is a major component of destination price, a country might become less price competitive not because of any rise in domestic price levels, but perhaps because of aviation fuel price rises. The 1991 crisis in The Gulf region has had this impact already, and it may yet get worse.

Tourism is an activity which can provide many benefits to a country. Each country, or destination within a country, has to undertake its own analysis of its comparative advantage. This analysis will provide the basis for policy formulation and related development planning. Although such analyses will be specific to countries, it may be possible to specify 3 models of general tourism development:

i) The first model relates to the developed countries where industry and industralisation is the main focus for development with tourism providing secondary economic activity, eg United States, United Kingdom, West Germany. Although tourism is seen as a secondary activity, it may be in fact the main activity within certain areas, eg Florida, Scotland, and also be supported by a high level of domestic tourism.
ii) The second model is where countries also rely on industry and agriculture to provide the main thrust for development but view tourism as an important contributor, particularly of foreign exchange, to the development effort. Countries such as Yugoslavia, India, Thailand, Kenya and China would be included in this group.
iii) The third model includes these countries where tourism dominates the economy, it is the main economic activity and the principal provider of government finance. Included in this group would be the Caribbean island nations, eg The Bahamas, Barbados, Pacific countries such as Fiji, Samoa, and Indian Ocean countries such as The Seychelles and The Maldives. This group of countries is characterised by small nation-states with very limited resources for development.

Each model includes a broad set of circumstances which are relevant to a country's level and stage of development. There will obviously be considerable variations between each country, but in all 3 models tourism is seen as having an input, and often a major input, to the development process. Although historically this input has been identified mainly in economic terms, in the next chapter it is argued that tourism's contribution to development should be regarded comprehensively, and not in relation to singular economic, social and environmental impacts.

References

1 Erbes R *International Tourism and the Economy of Developing Countries* 1973 OECD, Paris.

8 Impacts and implications of tourism in development strategy

The previous two chapters have examined the concept of tourism strategy and the case for tourism as part of development strategy. This chapter examines the ways in which tourism impacts on economies and societies.

If we consider the era of modern tourism to be characterised by the macro movements of people for leisure purposes, then this can be said to date from the decade of the 1950s. In that decade, recovery from the ravages of World War II provided opportunities for people to enjoy higher levels of income and paid holidays which, in combination with other factors, boosted international travel. As international tourism grew, it received more attention from governments, specialist organisations and analysts. The analytical studies on tourism can be categorised into three periods. The first period up to about the mid-1970s, saw much concentration on the economic impacts of tourism. Early studies by Bryden[1], Checci[2], Zinder[3] and Archer[4] were essentially economic analyses of tourism. The second period from about mid-1970s, saw the development of studies which were more critical of tourism's impact, particularly relating to its effects on people and societies. Studies by de Kadt[5], Smith[6], Turner and Ash[7] are examples. From the early 1980s onward much more attention has been given to the question of environmental issues in tourism. The Madrid conference[8] is an example.

The position in 1990 is that tourism has achieved recognition as a major economic activity not only on a global basis, but also at regional and at country levels. This recognition is not uncritical; investors in tourism both public and private sectors, realise that risk is inherent in the investment decision, and that short-term economic gains might be submerged by long-term social and environmental problems arising from investment in tourism. For tourism is a *people industry* and people travel with their preferences, prejudices and behavioural patterns. Cross-cultural conflicts, if not inevitable, are possible. Environmental degradation can arise from poor planning or over-crowding. For these, and many other reasons, the potential benefits and costs of investing in the tourist sector needs to be considered at the planning stage and not after the facility becomes operational. Fortunately, there are well-documented cases of good and poor tourism development from which we can learn. The purpose of this chapter is to examine what these impacts might be, and how we can learn form past experience to avoid replicating poor planning and development practice in the future. To facilitate exposition, examination of tourism's impacts will be related to the economy, society and environment, although in many cases impacts affect all three areas.

Economic impacts of tourism

The main economic impacts of tourism relate to foreign exchange earnings, contributions to government revenues, generation of employment and income, and contribution to regional development. The first two effects take place at the macro or national level, whereas the other 3 impacts occur at sub-national or regional levels. These effects are interrelated, but for analytical purposes it is useful to separate them.

Before examining these impacts it should be noted that with the exception of foreign exchange earnings, the other impacts can be generated by domestic tourism activity. Although domestic tourism does not earn foreign currency, encouragement of domestic tourism perhaps combined with legislation limiting or prohibiting foreign travel will save that amount of foreign exchange which would otherwise be spent for this purpose. As noted in the previous chapter, it is now unlikely that governments in developed countries would impose such legislation, but it is a common barrier to international travel in many developing countries where foreign exchange resources are scarce.

It is now generally accepted that international tourism constitutes one of the most significant of global trade flows. For reasons previously noted, precise estimates of tourism's economic worth are difficult to make. A study commissioned by American Express[9] indicated that in 1987 based on an analysis of over 200 countries and using 35 different international data sources it was estimated that

i) travel and tourism accounted for nearly US$2 trillion sales in 1987. To put this in perspective, if travel were a country, its Gross National Product (GNP) would rank fourth in the world after the United States ($4.5 trillion), in Soviet Union ($2.5 trillion), Japan ($2.4 trillion). Travel and tourism sales are larger than the GNP of West Germany and the United Kingdom combined.

ii) travel and tourism is the largest employer in most countries, providing jobs for one out of every 16 workers worldwide.
iii) travel and tourism gross output of nearly $2 trillion accounts for more than 5 per cent of all goods and services and 15 per cent of global service sector sales'.

The very substantial estimates revealed in the American Express study can be related to the fact that international tourism has two main impacts on countries' Balance of Payments – the trade and redistributive effects.

The trade effect is a characteristic of international tourism demand. The act of travel itself induces a trade effect. Most long-haul travellers travel by air; most aeroplanes are designed, manufactured, and sold by the United States. At the destination, the tourist might use accommodation owned and managed by non-residents. A German tourist visiting Sri Lanka might travel on Air Lanka using a DC 10 aircraft (made in the USA); stay in a foreign owned and managed hotel (Taj Group, India); and drink French wine, Scotch Whisky and eat Australian beef. To the tourist-receiving country these imports represent leakages; to the international economy they constitute trade opportunities and generate exports.

The redistributive effect of international tourism refers to the fact that most international tourists come from high-income developed countries, and spend part of their discretionary income in lower income countries by the purchase of holidays. In this way, some of the surplus spending power of the richer countries is through tourism, re-distributed to other countries, many of them being in the developing world. The relatively wealthy countries of Western Europe, North America, Japan, Australia and New Zealand, are major generators of tourists internationally and/or regionally. For a country like Japan with a high surplus on its Balance of Payments, encouraging residents to travel abroad is one means of reducing and redistributing this surplus.

At the level of the destination country, the economic impacts of tourism are usually categorised as follows:

Foreign exchange earnings

Foreign exchange earnings are the receipts of non-domestic currencies earned by selling goods and services to foreign tourists. It is useful to classify earnings into *hard*, ie convertible currencies and *soft* non-convertible currencies. A hard currency, eg US dollar, deutchmark, pound sterling, Swiss franc, is freely available, internationally acceptable, and can be exchanged without restriction. As these currencies are issued by the economically most advanced countries, they are most used in international trade. On the other hand, soft currencies are not freely available, and have severe limitations imposed on exchange outside the country of issue, eg Indian rupee.

Estimates of foreign exchange earnings from tourism are usually derived from sample *surveys of tourists* expenditure, and returns from tourism related activities, eg air fare payments. These estimates are found in the Travel Account of the Balance of Payments, and international fare payments in the Transportation Account. There are some serious methodological issued relating to the measurement of foreign exchange derived from tourism, not least being that estimates are given in gross and current terms. Gross estimates of earnings do not deduct the inputs (in foreign exchange) necessary to earn the foreign exchange; current estimates on a year-to-year basis do not take into account inflation or currency fluctuations. There are ways to overcome these problems, eg using constant price indicators and a foreign exchange deflator. Multiplier analysis and input-output procedures provide better estimates of net benefit. However, despite these technical problems, tourism's contribution to foreign exchange earnings is substantial; it is the main contributor in The Bahamas, India and Thailand, and the third ranked contributor in the United Kingdom.

Contribution to government revenues

Government revenue from the tourism sector many be categorised as being direct or indirect. Direct contributions arise from possibility of charging tax on incomes, both personal and company, generated by tourism employment and business. Indirect sources of revenue will comprise the range of taxes and duties levied on goods and services supplied to tourists. In many developing countries the identifiable labour force is small, with the majority of employment found in agriculture, often at a subsistence level. This low-level employment base means that direct taxation is not a major source of government revenue. In practice, in most developing countries government's revenues are accrued from indirect taxes. eg on crops, on land, on imports.

The ability of government to generate revenue by imposing high levels of taxation on personal and government incomes should be avoided. Excessive levels of taxation will be a disincentive to investors and might deter reinvestment. In some countries where tourism is a major contributor to government revenue, eg The Bahamas, Bermuda, no direct taxation on personal or company income is charged. Revenue is generated indirectly by a tax on goods and services.

There may not be clearly defined *tourism taxes*, ie goods and services bought by foreign tourists or domestic tourists. The 2 groups may be difficult to identify. Therefore, a bednight tax might be paid by all users of accommodation, as might airport departure taxes, general sales taxes, etc. In practice, governments will attempt to raise taxes on main areas of economic activity; where tourism is an important sector in the economy, it will be expected to generate its share of taxation revenue. Governments provide a wide range of services for the tourism sector and will expect a return on that investment and perhaps a surplus.

Employment and income generation

Employment generated by tourism can be either direct or indirect. Direct employment can be defined as jobs created specifically by the need to supply and serve tourists. An obvious example is the jobs created by the opening of a tourist hotel. As the hotel itself will have to buy-in certain services, eg laundry, taxis, etc, this will indirectly create jobs.

The disparate nature of tourism activity makes it difficult to estimate the employment impact. Even in developed economies such as the United Kingdom, the actual number of jobs *in tourism* is estimated. This problem is derived from the difficulty of defining the *tourism sector* and deciding what is to be included and excluded. In many countries, and certainly in developing countries, it may be necessary to undertake specific surveys to estimate employment generated by tourism.

The efficiency, ie cost-effectiveness of job creation in tourism is of interest, at least to the economic planner. Tourism is often described as a labour-intensive activity. At a simple level, this can be interpretated as meaning that per unit of capital employed, tourism creates more jobs than a similar unit of capital invested in another sector. This relationship is often expressed as a cost-per-job in one sector of employment compared with another. In those industries with large-scale operations or technologically sophisticated processes, large investments might create few jobs. An oil refinery is an example where heavy capital investment is required to process the oil, but generates relatively fewer jobs than a similar amount of investment in tourism or perhaps the agricultural sector; in the latter sectors, cost-per-job would be lower and labour-intensity higher.

In many developing countries with rapidly growing populations and high levels of unemployment, productivity of labour may not be a prime consideration. As labour is in abundant supply, is relatively cheap and tourism employment has a low skills threshold, the industry is often seen as a good source of employment opportunities. It should, however, be noted that tourism in many countries is a seasonal activity and this factor together with the initial low-skills jobs provided in tourism has been a continuing problem which can only be mitigated by long-term policy initiatives relating to manpower development and training.

The income effects of tourism are important as they are a direct effect of the level of tourism activity which, in turn, may stimulate other sectors of the economy. In developing countries, tourism-generated incomes are often higher than average levels of income. This situation has a number of implications. For the individual, tourism employment not only provides a higher income but often better working conditions and benefits compared with other sectors, eg agriculture. For the area economy, tourism may stimulate higher levels of economic activity and become a catalyst for growth. An example would be the island of Bali in Indonesia where tourism income has given the Balinese the highest levels of per capital income in the 27 Provinces which constitute the country.

The employment and income affects of tourism are interlinked; in turn, they are part of the total impact of tourism. Their singular importance is that they trigger the multiplier effect which enhances total economic benefit to the economy. Although economically important, it should be remembered they the type and location of employment in tourism will have social, and possible, cultural implications. The very fact of having a job in tourism may give rise to changes which are essentially social in nature. These changes can induce policy issues which may be critical to further development in the sector.

Regional development

The regional impact of tourism is often one of its main attractions to economic planners. It can make use of historical and cultural sites, eg Borobadur Temple complex in Java, Indonesia; scenic nature of a landscape, eg Scotland, and natural climate advantages, eg Gold Coast in Queensland, Australia, to provide a focus for development. Many of these locations have, for many reasons, few alternative economic development possibilities. In these examples, tourism generates income, employment and economic activity within a region, and often in so doing, help to sustain a community at an enhanced level of income.

Although in most countries governments encourage tourism for its economic benefits, at sub-national levels, other priorities might predominate. Tourism may be given priority in one region, eg Florida, but not in another, Wisconsin, because of its propensity to generate jobs and incomes. In the context of a developed country, from 1968 to 1984 approximately, the British government encouraged tourism because of its potential to earn foreign exchange (and to help to reduce the deficit on the Balance of Payments). Although this importance has not diminished, increasing emphasis is being given to the role of tourism as an employment and income generator in areas of the country where fewer economic development opportunities exist.

Despite the important economic impacts which tourism has, it is essentially a massive flow of individuals, a cross-border flow which will have important social and cultural effects on destination areas.

Social and cultural impacts of tourism

There is now a well developed literature on social and cultural impacts of tourism. Many research studies are highly specific, and may therefore be of more academic interest rather than of relevance to policymakers. However, experience in many different countries can be said to constitute a general phenomena relating to tourism. In many cases, the regularity with which these phenomenon are reported, allow policymakers to anticipate certain impacts from future developments in tourism.

It is easy to exaggerate impacts arising from tourism. For example, certain areas of a country may never be visited by tourists; tourist visits to very large countries such as India, tend to be concentrated in certain areas or circuits. Therefore, to refer to *the social and cultural impacts of tourism on India* must be an absurdity. Tourism tends to be localised and therefore, impacts tend to be localised initially. Whether these impacts cause changes, and whether these changes spread through society, will be influenced by a wide range of factors, eg size of country, general spread of tourism activity, basic cultural and religious strengths, etc.

It is unfortunate that many of the writers on social and cultural impacts have tended to react negatively to tourism development. These negative reactions should be viewed in the same way that economic disbenefits are – they are problems which require management solutions. They will not go away and might intensify. As tourism is a great international exchange of people, it is as important to plan for human reaction as it is for economic needs.

It is usual to regard the social and cultural impacts of tourism as comprising the non-economic aspects arising from tourism development. It is also usual to cite specific examples of these effects in relation to locations, regions and countries. Both dichotomies are artificial. For example, many of the social and cultural changes induced by tourism have definite economic costs, eg movement of labour from the agriculture sector to work in the tourism sector. These costs of transference would be enhanced if accompanied by an increase in urbanisation or wage-rate inflation. It should also be noted that growth in tourist arrivals in developing countries have provided general, and not only specific experience, of the impact of tourism on such countries. This collective general experience is important because it helps us to understand the nature of tourism as it impacts on the society and environment. Unfortunately, many of these changes are difficult to measure, and may not be entirely caused by tourism.

Closer study of this relationship has made us more aware of the social, cultural and environmental problems which can arise from tourism, and particularly from an over-rapid growth in visitor arrivals. Many of these problems can now be anticipated and therefore considered in relation to be policy and planning framework. It should, of course, be noted that many of these problems are not new. In the Caribbean, Asia, and Africa, there are many examples of newly-independent countries which have *inherited* mature tourist sectors, eg Jamaica, Barbados, and more recently, Zimbabwe may be mentioned. In these countries, many of the problems of the tourism sector are not of recent origin, and may cause particular difficulty in finding management solutions.

Despite these difficulties, governments have ultimately to find means of managing, if not completely eradicating these problems. This is particularly the case where tourism-related problems impact on the socio-cultural values of the society or on the environment. These wider concerns are the responsibility of government, and it may be that government is the only agent able to introduce required changes. Many of the social and cultural effects of tourism are portrayed as being essentially negative; studies by de Kadt[5] and O'Grady[10] have both detailed cases where tourism has made very serious changes in the structure, values, and traditions of societies. There is continuing debate as whether these changes are beneficial or not; the interests of society and the individual are not necessarily similar. There is little doubt, however, where international tourism is of any significance in a country, it does become a major *change-agent*.

It is not surprising that international tourism should induce such changes, because tourists usually remain in the host country for a very short time. They bring with them their traditions, values and expectations. They travel in what Eric Cohen[11] has termed an *ecological bubble* – a tourist infrastructure of facilities based on Western standards has to be created even in the poorest host country. This tourist infrastructure provides the mass tourist with the protective *ecological bubble* of his accustoms environment. In many countries, tourists are not sensitive to local customs, traditions, and standards. Offence is given without intent. In a sense, foreign visitors do not integrate into a society, but rather confront it. Where large numbers of tourists arrive in a country (often of one nationality) reaction is inevitable.

Reaction may take two forms; either a rejection of foreign tourists by locals, or an adoption of foreigner's behaviour patterns to constitute a social *demonstration effect.* In both cases problems will arise. An on-going point for discussion would be in which ways can tourists be made aware of local customs, traditions and *taboos*? Is the information process only a function of low volume tourism as for example in Western Samoa, Bhutan – or can it be adopted for high-volume visitor flows, eg India, Thailand?

When tourists enter the host country, they do not just bring their purchasing power and cause amenities to be set up for their use, they also, and above all, bring a different type of behaviour which can profoundly transform local social habits by removing and upsetting the basic and long-established values and patterns of behaviour of the host population. For example, hotel workers might have to attend shift working which effects religious observance.

During the tourist season, the resident population not only has to accept the effects of overcrowding, which may not exist for the remainder of the year, but they must often completely modify their way of life: increased work rhythm, dual activity, etc. and live in close contact with a different type of population, mainly urban, who are there simply for leisure. This *coexistence* is not always easy and often leads to social tension, zenophobia, particularly noticeable in very popular tourist areas or where the population, for psychological, cultural or social reasons, is not ready to be submitted to *the tourist invasion*.

An impact commonly expressed as the *demonstration effect* results from the close interaction of divergent groups of people, and manifests itself by a transformation of values. Most commonly it leads to changed social values resulting from raised expectations amongst the local population aspiring to the material standards and values of the tourists. Not unnaturally, changing social values lead to altered political values, sometimes with unsettling consequences. A decline in moral and religious values is also not uncommon and may show itself through increased crime levels. Not only are local attitudes changed, but the targets and opportunities for criminal activity are increased.

Tourism being, above all, a human activity, it is important to have the closest harmony between the attitudes of tourists and the behaviour of the local population. We are here treading on very delicate ground, where numerous qualitative parameters are involved: the socio-professional structures of the local population, the level of education and knowledge, the standard of living, their opinions and attitudes in the face of the tourist phenomenon and its cultural and institutional effects. What is certain is that the local population constitutes a human heritage which is just as important as the natural heritage and must, therefore, be protected.

Tourism may generate other social costs, often difficult to estimate, but which are no less serious for that reason. Mention can be made of the threat to traditional customs specific to each country, and sometimes to each region. (Although tourism may become the guarantor for the maintenance of certain original traditions which attract the holidaymaker). It is a question of protecting and maintaining the cultural heritage and dealing with a certain number of connected problems: the illegal trade in historic objects and animals, unofficial archaeological research, erosion of aesthetic values and of certain traditional know-how, disappearance of high-quality crafts, etc.

The commercialization of traditional cultural events may lead to the creation of pseudo-culture, ersatz folklore for the tourist, with no cultural value for the local population or the visitor. The same applies where the craftsman is concerned. The issue is the potential opposition between the economic and the cultural interests leading to culture being sacrificed for reasons of economics, ie creating an additional economic value at the price of losing a cultural value.

However, the exposure of resident populations to other cultures, due to tourism, would appear to be an irreversible process. It is often accompanied by an evolution in attitudes of mind, in tastes, in the judgement of values and may even lead of a certain decline in conservative attitudes – a further example of the *demonstration effect*. On a social level, planned tourism can favour contacts between holidaymakers and the local population, will encourage cultural exchanges and ethnic relations, will lead to friendly and responsible enjoyment and finally, will strengthen links between countries.

As noted above, international tourism, certainly more than domestic tourism, tends to confront a host community rather than integrate into it. There are many reasons for this. The main reason is that tourists are short-stay visitors carrying with them their own cultural norms and behaviour patterns. They are usually unwilling to change these norms for a temporary stay – and may be unaware that these norms are offensive or unacceptable to the resident host community.

A further difficulty can be the existence of a language barrier which itself may be a major factor limiting visitor understanding of host community manners and behavioural patterns. Language barriers create their own cocoon limiting social interchange between tourists and residents. These difficulties will create a problem, and gives rise to a need to provide some form of tourism *education* for visitor and host.

Perhaps the most difficult problem in identifying socio-cultural impacts is that they can take a very long time to emerge and be noticed. Unlike the economic effects of tourism which are readily seen, changes in society may be imperceptible but cumulative. It may also be very difficult to identify tourism as the cause of these changes as opposed to other influences, eg radio, newspaper, television. For example, is the *social demonstration effect* solely attributable to what tourists are seen to do? Or may it be influenced by general media reporting? If changes in society are evolutionary rather than revolutionary, then tourism analysts must have a system for monitoring these changes and reacting to them when necessary.

Some groups of tourists are more insensitive to local cultures than others. Often low-income, large group numbers based on cheap inexpensive tours can bring particular problems, eg British *lager-louts* visiting certain areas of Spain. This is not to hypothesise that all low income groups are badly behaved and insensitive to local traditions and custom. Certain ethnic groups might also exhibit characteristics which are unacceptable in a particular location or country, eg Japanese male *sex-tours* to Bangkok. Where problems are clearly associated with groups of tourists from a particular country or perhaps sent by a particular company, action should be taken to curb the problem.

One of the problems of changing the type of tourism activity is that tourists and residents often have a very different view of a country and its society. A country's tourism *image* may be the creation of a travel company, keen to stress those aspects of a country which it believes may persuade tourists to buy holidays in the destination. So what might be regarded as a *quaint* aspect of life by a tourist might be regarded as a symbol of *backwardness* by residents. Religious rites and ceremonies treated as a *holiday experience* by tourists can represent a fundamental aspect of life for residents. In a similar vein, alcohol, promiscuity, gambling, begging may be regarded differently by tourists and residents. There are only a few generalised examples of changes which can arise from tourism.

Attempts should be made to take into the planning process the socio-cultural dimension. It may be that in certain areas, tourism development should not be permitted. The concept of Tourism Development Zones should therefore include not only the tourism assets, potential and actual, of a location, but include a careful assessment of the proposed development on the local community. In the same way that environmental concerns are in integral part of planning for tourism, so should be the socio-cultural dimension. Many of the problems associated with socio-cultural effects might be mitigated if economic benefits remain largely within the community.

The evolution of community tourism as expressed by Murphy[12] is an important development for it recognises that to be substainable in the long-term, tourism has to be acceptable to the community within which it takes place. More attention is now being given by planners to this aspect of development, and this is one approach to minimising the negative social effects of tourism and to increase its general acceptability within destinations.

Environmental impacts of tourism

Environment is usually narrowly defined to refer solely to the physical environment which can be sub-divided into natural and build segments. The natural environment is what exists from nature – climate, flora and fauna, topography, etc with the built environment including all man made features, eg the Taj Mahal, St Paul's Cathedral, the Great Pyramids. However, it is important to accept that the analysis of the environment in a comprehensive sense should also include socio-cultural and economic factors. It is often difficult and not desirable to examine these features as separate components.

Environmental issues are now central to planning; very few projects are developed without an Environmental Impact Analysis being made. More attention is being given at the planning stage to preventing bad design rather than having to undertake remedial actions when the project is operational. The quality of the environment is a major issue on a global basis, and for tourism which depends critically on this input, it is of paramount importance. There is a long catalogue of environmental damage caused by poor design, location or scale of projects; tourism developments are not the only offenders.

Environmental damage caused to, and sometimes by tourism developments, are to be found all over the world:

i) Water pollution: discharge of sewerage effluent into beach and bay at Pattaya, Thailand.
ii) Visual pollution: high-rise hotel developments at Waikiki Beach, Hawaii.
iii) Congestion: Kutar Beach and tourism area, Bali, Indonesia.
iv) Land use pollution: ribbon development along Spanish coastal areas.
v) Ecological disruption: to animal breeding by uncontrolled access to game parks, Africa.

To these common examples can be added the problems of litter, traffic fumes and over-crowding which afflict many tourist sites both rural and urban. To a large degree these problems have been caused by the too rapid increase in tourist arrivals which puts pressure on infrastructure and the environment. In most developed countries there is extensive planning legislation and controls to curb the worst excesses of developers, but some projects do proceed. In the developing countries which often do not have a coherent and comprehensive planning framework, the problems are more acute.

Tourism, however, can make positive contributions to environmental improvement; four examples exemplify this point.

i) The interest which tourists have in the natural and built environment often allows these areas to be protected and managed. There are many examples in developed countries of areas being designated as *national parks* or *areas of outstanding natural beauty*. These areas are so designated to control access and use and to ensure that they are sustainable in the future. Similar reasoning applies to the conservation of animal species and to the built environment, eg Stonehenge, England.
ii) The improvement in environmental quality benefits both visitor and resident. Pedestrianisation of many urban attractions has benefitted access to visitor and increased the amenity of the resident.
iii) Improvements in infrastructure for tourists often *spills-over* to residents. The Adriatic Highway in Yugoslavia improved tourist access to the South but also improved transport links for residents and industry.
iv) Revenue generated by tourism allows funding of conservation and maintenance to facilities and amenities which otherwise might deteriorate.

In all cases, prevention is cheaper than cure! As part of tourism development planning, environmental considerations must be given a high level of priority. In some environmentally sensitive and fragile areas, development may be prohibited. A central consideration is the carrying-capacity of a destination in relation to visitor use and the development of facilities. Tourism may be an important means to achieve conservation, for without a good quality environment, tourists many choose to visit alternative destinations.

The politics and economics of environmental development and protection are a major subject. Sufficient to note here that in examining the impacts of tourism on a destination or project, the aspects of economic, socio-cultural and environmental impacts should be regarded as components of a larger concern. The Manila Declaration of the World Tourism Organisation, accepted in 1980[12] notes the link between national and cultural resources in developing tourism, and the need to conserve these resources for the benefit of tourists and residents of the tourism area. The Joint Declaration of the World Tourism Organisation and the United Nations Environment Programme stated 'The protection, enhancement and improvement of the various components of man's environment are amongst the fundamental conditions for the harmonious development of tourism. Similarly, rational management of tourism many contribute to a large extent to protecting and developing the physical environment and cultural heritage as well as improving the quality of life...'[13].

The quotation implies the need for comprehensive approach to the development and management of tourism at the destination. Without this approach, environmental degradation will occur and sustaining tourism resources in the long term may not be possible.

References

1 Bryden J M *Tourism and Development*, 1973 Cambridge University Press.

2 Checci & Co *A Plan for Managing Tourism in the Bahama Islands*, Washington DC, 1969.

3 Zinder, H & Associates, *The Future of Tourism in the Eastern Caribbean*, Washington DC, 1969.

4 (a) Archer B H *The Impact of Domestic Tourism*, Economics Research Unit, 1973 University of Wales, Bangor.

(b) Archer B H *The Gwynedd Multipliers* Economics Research Unit, 1973 University of Wales, Bangor.

5 de Kadt, E (ed) *Tourism – Passport to Development?*, 1979 Oxford University Press.

6 Smith V L *Hosts and Guest: An Anthropology of Tourism,* 1977 University of Pennsylvania Press.
7 Turner L and Ash J, *The Golden Hordes*, 1975 Constable, London.
8 World Tourism Organisation and United Nations Environment Programme, *Workshop on Environmental Aspects of Tourism,* 1983.
9 American Express Company, *The Contribution of the World Travel and Tourism Industry to the Global Economy,* 1987 Executive Summary.
10 O'Grady R *Third World Stop-over,* 1981 World Council of Churches, Geneva.
11 Cohen E *Towards a Sociology of International Tourism,* 1972 Social Research 39 (1), 172.
12 Murphy P E *Tourism: A Community Approach,* 1985 Methuen.
13 World Tourism Organisation and United Nations Environment Programme *Joint Declaration on Tourism in the Environment,* 1982, Madrid.

9 Tourism in development – four case studies

The previous chapters have set out the reasons for, and the role of, tourism in the development process. In this chapter four brief case studies of *tourism-in-action* are presented. All four countries are part of the developing world, chosen because they represent in their different ways examples which are relevant to other countries. The countries are:

i) India: an example of a large country which is a well established tourism destination.
ii) Nigeria: an example of a large country – with limited tourism development, considerable potential but almost unrecognised as a tourist destination.
iii) Morocco: a well established short-haul destination for European tourists.
iv) Indonesia: a very large archipelagic country with outstanding tourism potential and now in the process of establishing a tourism development strategy.

In presenting case studies for these four countries, attention will be focussed on four main points: some background to the countries themselves; the economic structure; policy issues relevant to tourism; and the role that tourism has in development strategies. In relation to tourism policy it should be noted that policy might be explicit or implicit. Where policy is explicit it is usually formulated into legislation, published and therefore is generally available for reference. Although there may be problems relating to the implementation of policy, there are established guidelines for action. Implicit policies are usually *ad hoc* actions which are not available in written form. Government, or its agent might take action to support and develop tourism, but does not have a coherent policy. For example, in the United Kingdom, there is no national tourism policy. Government, by financing national tourist boards, by employment initiatives, and through ministerial statements obviously supports the development of tourism – but there is no explicit policy.

In developing countries, because of their acute development needs and limited resources, it is usual to find formal statements of development objectives usually set out in 5-year development plans. Where tourism is an important sector in the economy, a set of development objectives is usually included in the national plan. It should be remembered however, that the existence of a plan is no guarantee of its implementation: the frustration felt by many economic planners is summarized in the following quotation: 'In developing countries plans are formulated and never launched, others are launched but abandoned thereafter, still others are executed but fall far short of achieving their targets. In most plans there is a gap between the formulation and implementation of plans. This condition has led planners even to allege and doubt, if at all plans are really meant to be implemented and not just to serve the politicians'.[1]

India

The country

India, by an international standard, is a very large country. It has a surface area of 3,288,000 square kilometers and an estimated population in mid-1988 of approximately 796 million people, of which only 27 per cent live in urban areas. The economic patterns of India has attracted much analysis and international attention. Although categorised as an agrarian economy, the country has made substantial progress in developing its industries, and has some high technology sectors of the economy. It is a democratic, federal union, with the individual states retaining a considerable degree of political and development autonomy.

The economy

The bulk of India's population is based on the rural areas and the vagaries of monsoon and harvest are a constant threat to the survival of its citizens. Although having a fairly wide-spread economic base, eg exports of textiles, manufactured goods, intermediate products, the country faces the usual problems of export restrictions by tariffs and quotas. A major problem is the shortage of foreign exchange for investment purposes. These pressures are made more acute by the rapid increase in the population, political instability, and continuing problems with Pakistan.

Tourism policy issues

Tourism has a long-established importance in India. In the post war era, the Sargent Committee[2] set out some major guidelines for tourism development. In 1981, Som N Chib, perhaps the most distinguished of Indian tourism authorities, presented a precis of Indian tourism objectives in a lecture[3] in which he identified four major factors:

a) tourism is a unifying force nationally and internationally fostering better understanding through travel.
b) tourism helps to enrich, preserve and retain India's world view and life style through cultural expressions and heritage in all its manifestations.
c) tourism brings socio-cultural benefits to the community and the states in terms of employment opportunities, income generators, foreign exchange earnings and in general, human habitant improvement.
d) tourism provides an opportunity to the youth of the country through international and domestic tourism to understand the aspirations and viewpoints of others and this brings about greater national integration and cohesion.

What is striking about this summary is the importance that India places on tourism as a nationally unifying force, and with considerable significance being given to cultural heritage. Chib's lecture was confirmed in its detail by a statement made to the Indian parliament by the then Minister of State for Tourism and Civil Aviation, Mr Khursid Alam Khan[4]. The main features of a tourism policy were:

a) to undertake development of tourism, and to take into account the needs – and potentials – of rural areas, and economically disadvantaged areas.
b) to facilitate youth travel to foster national integration and identity.
c) to take account of domestic tourists needs of the country by providing cheap accommodation, particularly at places of pilgrimages.
d) to broaden the market base for international visitors to India.
e) to encourage domestic and private sector investment in tourism by means by incentives.
f) to conserve and manage the cultural heritage of the country.
g) to devote resources to manpower development and training.

To support these policies the Indian government has enacted a substantial volume of legislation. It has also introduced specific organisations to implement policies. At the federal level, the Indian Ministry of Tourism is the highest authority responsible for the management of Indian tourism at home and overseas. Planning of tourism is done on a 5 yearly cycle taking into account an annual rolling revision to adjust targets and meet contingencies. Planning includes all phases of tourism and this is then integrated into the national economic development plan. To implement policies, overseas promotion is channelled through the Indian Department of Tourism whereas the Indian Tourism Development Corporation operates certain tourism services, eg hotels, resorts, transport, and has a major liaison function with the private sector at both national and state levels.

Role of tourism

Tourism in India is still a highly concentrated activity with the Agra-Jaipur-Delhi so-called *Golden Triangle* remaining a major cultural attraction. However, changes in aviation policies permitting charter flights into selected airports, eg Goa, Kerella States, have tapped a new beach market segment for India. In 1988 Government figures show 1.6 million international arrivals with $1.5 billion receipts. The foreign exchange earnings from tourism are a major input to the Indian development effort. With the exception of the visiting friends and relatives (VFR) market generated from Pakistan and Bangladesh, the substantial proportion of India's tourists come from Europe and the Americas.

Conclusion

India has a clearly defined policy for tourism[5] backed by specialist institutions charged with responsibility to implement policies. Government, at federal and state levels cooperate to coordinate development and to make best use of available resources. There are limited funds available for development, but it is noticeable that India has emphasised the importance of domestic, and particularly youth tourism, as one means of forging national identity in a very large and diverse country. The problem facing tourism planners in India is to select developments from a very wide range of touristic possibilities. Selectivity has to be the key approach to avoid wasting resources. The administrative restructuring of the tourism sector in India[6] will provide a more streamlined organisational arrangement which should further improve the effectiveness of tourism planning and administration.

Nigeria

The country

Nigeria is one of the largest and most highly populated countries in Africa with a land area of 924,000 square kilometers and an estimated population in 1988 of 105 million[7]. Nigeria is largely an exporter of semi-manufactured goods, limited range of textiles and raw materials, and substantially depends on oil for its main source of export earnings.

The economy

Although recognised as having perhaps one of the best potentials for development in Africa, for various reasons Nigeria has failed to achieve either steady or substantial economic growth. Plagued by the problems of the civil war (1967–70) and by successive replacement of civilian governments by military governments, the country has been characterised by serious political instability. The economic goals of development have been frustrated by poor planning, poor management and by an inability to make productive use of its oil revenues. Tourism is now seen by the federal government as one means of diversifying the national and some state economies, by generating income and employment.

Tourism policy issues

The first positive effort to develop tourism in Nigeria might be traced to the Advisory Committee on the Promotion of the Tourism Industry in Nigeria which reported in 1959[8]. This *ad hoc* Committee involved a group of American travel agents to tour the country to comment and advise on tourism development possibilities. Most of the recommendations related to the need to concentrate development in selected sites and to improve infrastructural facilities and tourist services at these locations. The poor quality of infrastructure was noted and the absence of a federal agency to encourage and coordinate development. It was recommended that a Nigerian Tourist Association be founded, financed by subvention from the public and private sectors: this was done in 1962[9]. Unfortunately, due to a poorly organised private sector and underfunding by the federal government, the Nigerian Tourist Association was ineffective. It was replaced in 1976 by a Nigerian Tourist Board[10].

The policy objectives for Nigerian tourism are set out in the Nigerian Tourism Act 1976 and may be summarized as follows:

a) the Board should be responsible for the determination of overall policy and for operational, financial and economic programmes.
b) the Board was to recommend a land-use policy for tourism.
c) to established necessary subsidiary organisations to achieve tourism objectives.

In practice, the Nigerian Tourism Board has been unable to develop the tourism sector, largely because it is underfunded and has a limited authority base to stimulate developments. At the federal level it is on an inferior level to the main economic ministries, and at state level, the state tourism committees seem to have had limited impact. It is interesting to contrast this situation to India which is also a large, federal country. The main differences would appear to be that in India the tourism sector has been given an organisational structure, legislative support and appropriate levels of funding to achieve established goals. Nigeria has none of this and also suffers from major and continuing underfunding.

Role of tourism

Tourism is not an important sector in the Nigerian economy for the reasons noted above. It is a large country with tourism potential but suffering from severe infrastructural deficiencies, lack of a political will to develop the sector accompanied by a lack of adequate funding. It is difficult to estimate the real contribution of tourism to the economy. Nigerian Tourist Board figures for 1989 estimate 835,000 tourist arrivals generating receipts of $107 million. A startling figure is the estimated $205 million expenditure by Nigerians travelling outside the country, providing a net deficit on the Travel Account. There are no estimates available for employment generated by tourism.

Conclusion

The tourism sector in Nigeria is a good example of benign neglect. Although government has created a legislative structure for tourism, it is ineffective. There is a lack of specific policy and adequate funding, with little or no coordination between the federal and state levels. The tourism potential of the country has not been assessed since 1976 when the African Development Bank was commissioned to survey it. The Nigeria experience clearly demonstrates that political instability and tourism are not good bed-mates. A policy in itself would do little to overcome image problems associated with political upheaval. The future challenge for Nigeria is take lessons from tourism developments elsewhere, perhaps India, and provide a framework for positive and sustained development in the future.

Morocco

The country

Morocco is a country of 24 million people, situated in the North-Western part of the African continent and bordered by both the Mediterranean Sea and the Atlantic Ocean. It is only a short distance from the European mainland with Spain being only 15 kilometers from its coast.

The economy

Morocco has a well diversified economy although it remains an overwhelmingly agricultural economy. The development of agriculture and the export of agricultural produce has made Morocco virtually self-sufficient in food. Much of the industrial development in the country is associated with the products of the agricultural sector. Handcrafts and the traditional crafts of copper, silver and leather-working, continue to be an important area of employment which, in recent years, has been stimulated by demand from the tourism sector.

Like most developing countries Morocco is faced with a rapidly increasing population with the current population of 24 million forecast to increase to about 32 million by the year 2,000. In an attempt to stimulate economic growth and create employment, the Government is following a policy of liberalisation to stimulate investment and activity by the private sector. It is hoped that liberalisation policies will encourage exports, tourism and the important remittances from Moroccan workers abroad.

Tourism policy issues

The main impetus for developing tourism in the 1960s came from the Government. Much of the investment in infrastructure and management of the hotel sector was done by Government or its agents. Since 1983 the Government has adopted increasingly a role as enabler for development relying mainly on the private sector to provide the necessary development impetus.. The Government has, over the last two decades, given tourism an increasingly important role in the economy. The current National Development Plan 1988–92 focuses on a number of targets:

a) to create new tourism development areas with a better regional spread of projects.
b) to create a wider spread of holiday products but to avoid problems relating to overcrowding at specific destinations.
c) to reduce the effects of seasonality in the North and South of Morocco.
d) to meet the growing competition from adjacent Mediterranean countries by ensuring the country remains a high-quality destination.
e) to develop new markets in the United States, Japan and the Far East.

An important feature of this development plan is that the private sector is expected to finance 52 per cent of the proposed funding. Appropriate training and the provision of training facilities are provided for, as is new legislation to encourage private domestic and foreign investment in tourism. Despite the actions of government and the private sector, much remains to be done, particularly in overseas promotion. Morocco is in direct competition with Tunisia for short-haul tourists from mainland Europe. Countries like Spain, Greece, Yugoslavia and Turkey compete in the same market segment. Although Morocco has more up-market offerings based on the Imperial Cities circuit it is still much regarded as a beach destination by European tourists; as part of its policy, it is also trying to broaden its image.

Role of tourism

In the Moroccan economy tourism contributes approximately 5 per cent of Gross Domestic Product (GDP) and about 7–10 per cent of earnings of foreign currency. International tourism arrivals in 1989 were 2.5 million with international tourism receipts being $1.1 billion[12]. There is an ambitious target for expansion of visitor arrivals in 1988-92 of 12 per cent per annum. Current estimates are that the tourism sector employs 150,000 Moroccans. Again, in a country with a wide range of tourist attractions, future emphasise will be given to using tourism to stimulate regional development.

Tourism is now the second main earner of foreign currency after remittances from Moroccans working abroad. The Government obviously intends to continue to support the sector to assist in achieving regional development and wider economic diversification.

Conclusion

Over the last 20 years Morocco has made important developments in its tourism sector. To a large extent this is a result of positive government action encouraging laision as a means of achieving economic diversification and regional development. There are still problems to overcome. Land for tourism development is not always available and when it is, can be very expensive. There is a need to attract more foreign investment which the new incentive legislation may help to overcome. Seasonality remains a problem in some areas and this might be ameliorated by better marketing or finding new markets. There is also some need for the Moroccan National Tourism Officer to have its powers of intervention in the tourism sector increased, particularly related to the supervision of projects.

However, Morocco is a good example of a country competing for tourists in what must be one of the most competitive markets in the world – the European short-haul. It has established an organisational structure and legislation to support that structure in an attempt to develop tourism to meet the economic challenges of the next decades.

Indonesia

The country

Indonesia forms part of the world's largest archipelago covering 1.9 million square kilometers, encompassing over 13,000 islands and stretches approximately 2,500 kilometers from West to East. The estimated population in 1990 is over 176 million people with 65 per cent of the population being on the three islands of Java, Bali and Madura. Administratively, the country is divided into 27 Provinces and special territories. The climate is tropical with a rainy season from November to April and a dry season from May to October.

The economy

The Indonesian economy, like many developing countries, is dependent on the agricultural sector for most of its employment. Exports of oil, tropical hardwoods and rubber have been the main contributors to export earnings. Since 1965 the government has achieved a reputation for political stability, and despite strong centralist policies, progress has been slow but steady. In the 1980s the government was encouraging diversification in economic terms of investment and employment. The government was particularly mindful not to become overdependent on oil exports as Nigeria had been. As a member of the Association of South East Asia Nation (ASEAN) group, Indonesia subscribed to regional policies. In relation to the economy there are seven main concerns:

a) the need to diversify the economy.
b) to improve the infrastructure.
c) to find more jobs for the growing workforce.
d) to improve domestic transport links.
e) to attract more private sector funding from domestic and foreign sources.
f) to generate more development in the regions, and
g) to increase foreign exchange earnings to meet existing external debt servicing obligations.

The economy is planned by a series of Five Year Development Plans (Repelita) with the current plan being for 1989–93. Tourism is being emphasised as one means of combating the problems noted above.

Tourism policy issues

As yet, Indonesia does not have an explicit policy for tourism development, but rather a series of actions which aim to develop the sector. Economic targets for tourism are set out in the Repelita. The main issues currently facing the Indonesian government arise from dynamism rather than stagnation in the tourism sector:

a) visitor arrivals are increasing at the rate of 25 per cent per annum[13].
b) over 60 per cent of all visitors visit Bali, which has given rise to major environmental, social and physical problems.
c) very limited development of tour circuits within Indonesia.
d) need to improve infrastructure, accommodation, and availability of trained manpower to meet needs of *Visit Indonesia Year 1991*.
e) need to broaden the market's perception of the attractions and locations of attractions within the country.

To a large extent, the problem of Indonesia's diversified attractions is similar to that of India; a surplus of attractions and destinations with decisions having to be taken on priority developments. Within the international market place, Indonesia is still relatively unknown; despite the homogeneity of tourist attractions within the ASEAN region, Indonesia received only 9 per cent of foreign visitor arrivals to the regions in 1989.

The Government of Indonesia, supported by the United Nations Development Programme, is currently formulating a development strategy for the tourist sector. Amongst the issues noted above the question of a marketing strategy is vital. Indonesia through its

Directorate General of Tourism, wants to emphasise its cultural aspect in future tourism development; it does not want to be sold only as a beach resort destination. Although recognising the international image and reputation of Bali, it wants to avoid the worst excesses of over-development on the island, and use it as a spring-board for other destinations – *Bali and Beyond* is the marketing slogan. However, in such a large country with many attractions, the ability to publicise these attractions abroad, and to support development by reliable transport links, are major problems.

Tourism and the economy

The targets for tourism set out in Repelita V 1989–93 have mainly been set on the basis of historic trends; the target for 1989 was 1 million visitors, spending on average US $75 per day with an average 10 days length of stay. The main generating countries for Indonesia are Australia, Singapore and Japan, all hard currency generators. It appears that by the end of Repelita V the visitor arrivals figure of 2.5 million, will be easily exceeded and the per day spend of $150 approximated. It is not so clear that the length of stay target will be met. It is however expected that tourism will maintain if not improve its ranking as the fourth main earner of foreign exchange.

Great emphasise is being placed on tourism absorbing the rapid increase in the labour force. The Government already operates two Hotel and Tourism Training Institutes in Bali and Bandung, and a third is proposed. Emphasis on training is supported by a series of internationally funded projects aimed at improving labour standards.

Government has indicated its intention to promote development in the Eastern part of Indonesia. This area has very considerable tourism potential and could provide the required stimulus to economic diversification if the problems of infrastructure and transport can be overcome. Indonesia provides a good example of the regional development possibilities of tourism.

Conclusion

Although Indonesia does not yet have a formal tourism policy, government actions and decisions have created an implicit policy. There are very clear indications that government intends to use tourism to meet some of its economic problems and also its aspirations. There are many difficulties to be faced, not least the distance from its secondary markets in Europe and the United

States, its desire to develop itself as a cultural destination, and the problems related to a rapid expansion of visitor arrivals.

Very much like India and Morocco, the government is now encouraging private sector initiatives in tourism, with the government seeing its role as a minor partner. Indications are that this policy is beginning to work, for example with much of the rapid expansion of accommodation facilities in Jakarta and Bali being funded by Indonesian private sector funds. However, despite the encouragement of the private sector, government retains control over the type of tourism to be developed and is very conscious of the need to protect destinations physically, socially and environmentally.

References

1 United Nations *Guidelines for Development Planning: Procedure, Methods and Techniques*, 1987 Department of Technical co-operation for Development, New York, p 86.
2 Sargent J *Report and Recommendations of an Investigation in Potentialities for Developing Tourist Traffic to India* 1946
3 Chib S N *Perspectives on Indian Tourism* 1981 Sander Patel Memorial Lecture, New Delhi.
4 Khan K A *Indian Tourism Policy*; statement and presentation to Lok Sabho and Rayja Sabha 1982 November 3rd.
5 Indian Ministry of Tourism and Civil Aviation, *7th Five Year Plan for Tourism 1985–1990*, 1985 New Delhi.
6 Government of India: *Report of the National Committee on Tourism*, 1988 Planning Commission, New Delhi.
7 World Tourism Organisation, *Compendium of Tourism Statistics*, 1984–1988, 1989 10th edition, Madrid.
8 Government of Nigeria, Sessional Paper No 5, 1959 Federal Ministry of Commerce and Industry, Lagos.
9 Government of Nigeria, Government White Paper on Tourism, 1962 Lagos.
10 Government of Nigeria, Decree No 54 establishing Nigerian Tourism Board, 1976 Federal Ministry of Trade and Commerce, Lagos.
11 Ministry of Tourism *Strategy and Perspectives on the Development of the Tourism Sector* 1989
12 World Tourism Organisation, 1989: op cit 1989.
13 Government of Indonesia 1989 Central Bureau of Statistics, Jakarta.

Part III: Administrative structure for tourism development

Leonard Lickorish

10 Roles of government and the private sector

The essential tourist *product* consists of two elements – a desired satisfaction be it business or pleasure, for example relaxing on a beach or attending a conference; at an acceptable destination: city, resort or countryside. Many services combine to provide the total product but the destination itself clearly has a vital role to play, and in the visitor's mind represents the whole appeal at least at the stage of deciding on and planning the journey.

Usually there is no single *destination* owner other than the community as a whole and its representative the local government eg municipality. Thus the destination *guardian* must be the local public authority. In turn the role of the local authority in tourism is a very special and professional one. However, the authority's purpose in life is to care for the interests of the resident community, who can vote the controllers or local councillors in and out of office. Tourists in contrast make up the mobile or *temporary* community. They have no vote but their economic and social impact on the residents may be very significant, affecting their environment, prosperity, and indeed their whole lives. Tourists have their own power through the market place, deciding whether to come and spend their money buying the local products or take their custom elsewhere.

These points may seem simple and self evident, but they represent the background to development and are often ignored in the policy and planning process. The public authority has a dual role in tourism whether at the national or local level. In the first place it is the guardian and regulator, setting the conditions for development. It must introduce and implement legislation affecting such essential matters as public health and safety, the environment, and in recent years consumer protection within the free and fair competition of a well organised market economy. These tasks are part of the public authority's role in regulating and stimulating industry and commerce for the benefit of the local community.

In principle, the market economy should ensure development of trade and industry with maximum prosperity, without the intervention of government, once favourable conditions for free trade have been set. In practice this may be difficult to achieve if for example foreign competitors are aided or subsidised in their business. Specifically in the case of tourism the government authority must act as the representative of the destination itself and in so doing may become an operator as well as a regulator. The tourist trade is made up of a large number of competing services and businesses in transport, accommodation, catering, entertainment and many other personal services. Many will be small businesses. No single business could or should act for the whole area. They are not in charge of the scenery, the environment and many of the *natural* visitor attractions. The public authority is responsible for such elements in the tourist product. It may be a major operator, providing many *public* facilities, parks and gardens, recreation services such as swimming pools, tennis and even golf courses, camping, car parking sites, and often local transport. It may build and operate conference and exhibition halls, theatres, art galleries and other attractions. In addition it must be the guardian of the image, and assume responsibility for marketing, welcome and hospitality services such as information bureaux. The range of these essential services is considerable and costly to provide.

Usually therefore the public sector will be an operator, investor and trader, and entrepreneur as well as a marketer, and in addition the strategic planner for long term development. It will be the regulator or umpire for trade and commerce at the destination, local or national.

What does this mean in practice? At both national and local levels there must be good communication and co-operation and a sensible degree of direction and devolution of functions. Generally most trading, specific development and the provision of services including information should be left to local enterprise and initiative. There will be services which are needed to enhance the whole but either not directly profitable or not commercial. Clearly infrastructure provision such as roads, lighting, drains, waste collection etc must be public concerns. There will be many other functions which should be organised on a community basis: marketing, welcome and hospitality services, festivals and fairs for example, which all need a collective effort.

Tourism policy

In such cases the public authority will need to provide leadership and accept a vital advisory role establishing the machinery for co-operation and collective action with the private sector.

Government at national level, and the local authority at the specific destination level, will need an explicit rather than an implicit tourism policy which must be clearly stated. This will depend on the degree of past and present tourist development. It must clearly indicate the intended strategy for development and be formulated after full consultation with the trades as well as the resident population. This will be the basis for the national and local tourist plans which must be linked. Of course, in a free society the authority can opt out, but even in such cases an assessment should be made of costs and benefits forgone as well as consequences of unplanned and unexpected results. In this age of mobility travel will not stop, but its unplanned incidence could be damaging adding to the cost of lost opportunities in attracting compatible and prosperous travel trade. In fact government cannot escape involvement in tourism since the size and potential of the movement increasingly affects all aspects of community life, not least the outward flow of residents to foreign destinations, exporting their wealth and removing the benefits of visitor movement.

Travel movement increasingly affects most aspects of community life. If there is no overall tourism policy each department or agency of government will react to the incidence of tourism according to their own brief or objectives. The decisions are likely to be politically directed to meet the needs and wishes of the resident population alone. This will result in at best inadequate, and at worst prejudicial, programmes in the tourism field since the case for visitor needs will not be taken into account, nor the effects of visitor traffic on the location.

It is surprising in view of the economic and social importance of tourism in most developed countries that Governments in general give low priority to the trade in policies, and until recently rarely set out an explicit policy statement spelling out its role and the national objectives. The extracts from recent reports will illustrate this weakness. Even the European Community (EC) came late to tourism with the first official policy reports not made until 1986.

It seems a paradox that Government regards the trade as a business mainly for the private sector and for free competitive enterprise, yet the mechanics of visitor servicing need a public and private sector partnership, and the private sector cannot play its role effectively unless Government intentions and trading conditions are satisfactory and publicly known.

There have been some fundamental changes in policy over the years. While there has been a general practice of supporting international marketing for the national destination, and attempts to use tourism flows to support or prop up some national problem area or deficiency: lack of foreign exchange, regional regeneration or job creation; overall policy formulation has been the exception rather than the rule in the industrialised countries. The lack of central action has in many cases been compensated by action at the regional and local level, but with uneven results, and often handicapped by the exclusion of tourism considerations in transport policies.

Policy formulation

It must be a prime task of the destination public authority (National or local government to initiate destination policy formulation in the following basic stages:

1. Review of present trade and its recent evolution, note stage in growth cycle and changing trends.
2. Strength and Weakness (SWOT) Analysis.
3. Product – Market Match: identify broad market opportunities and compare with resource and product capacity, note constraints and ability to overcome.
4. Select priorities and examine cost benefit, including options, if any.
5. Formulate Policy options and communicate to:
   a. private and operating sector;
   b. other agencies of government, local or national, concerned;
   c. public (residents).
6. Review policy with input from 5. and set Objectives and Targets.
7. Prepare Marketing and Development Plan, and seek consultation on implementation as at 5.
8. Establish Monitoring process to measure performance against objectives.

The following summaries of public sector policies will give an indication of their character.

The Tourism Policy of the European Community and the related objectives were set out in 1986. They are:

1. to facilitate and promote tourism in the Community;

2. IC to improve its seasonal and geographic distribution;
3. to make better use of the Community financial instruments eg. the European Regional Development Fund (ERDF);
4. to provide better information and protection for visitors;
5. to improve the working conditions of persons employed in the tourism industry;
6. to provide more complete information on the sector and set up consultation and coordination between the Commission and member states.

An Explicit Tourism Policy for Switzerland was not adopted officially until 1979. Government considered the Swiss Tourist Industry as largely a matter for the private sector. Government intervention was limited to help for seasonal hotels, some infrastructure financing and funding for promotion by the Swiss National Tourist Office.

The *Conception Suisse du Tourisme* set objectives for society, the economy and the environment. The aim was to encourage a competitive and efficient tourism sector with the intention of both improving the position of the tourist in terms of choice and of the country and regions as a whole. The objectives can be summarised in the following chart.

A full list of the objectives of *La Conception Suisse du Tourisme* appears as an integral part of the report itself. Space does not permit the inclusion of all of these here and they are summarised in Figure 10.1.

Figure 10.1 List of objectives of La Conception Suisse duTourisme

LA CONCEPTION SUISSE DU TOURISME

GLOBAL OBJECTIVE

To guarantee optimal satisfaction of the needs of tourists and individuals from all walks of life in effectively grouped facilities and through conservation of the environment.

SECONDARY OBJECTIVES

SOCIAL	*ECONOMIC*	*ENVIRONMENTAL*
Create the best possible social conditions for locals and tourists	Encourage a tourist industry that is both competitive and efficient	Ensure the relaxing quality of both the countryside and man -made attractions

INTERMEDIATE AND PARTIAL OBJECTIVES

10 more objectives	*11 more objectives*	*8 more objectives*
E.G. more participation from locals	E.G. optimise the operation and structure of the industry	E.G. develop facilities in harmony with the environment

Source: Horwath Consultants

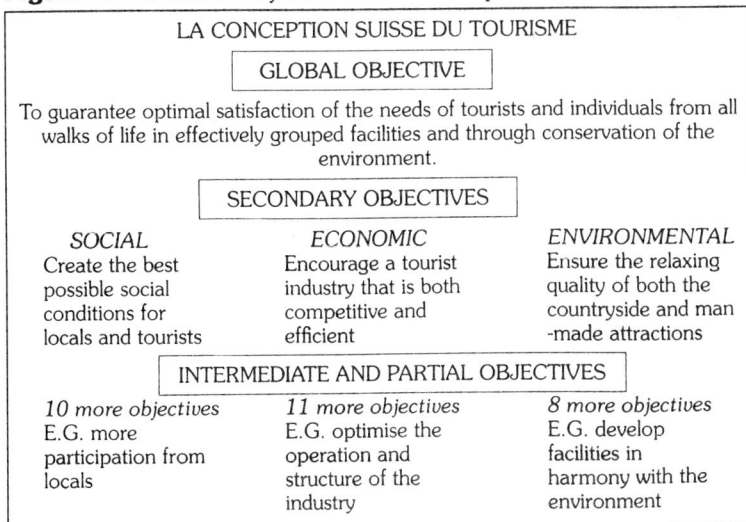

In Britain the government has been reluctant to publish an overall Tourism policy issuing *guidelines* to the statutory agencies (the British Tourist Authority and the Tourist Boards). However in 1985 a senior cabinet Minister, Lord Young, took an active interest in tourism and instituted an annual report on tourism. The following extract from the 1985 report[1] illustrates the attitude to policy and is a clear statement of the Government role at that time:

> 2. It may be asked why the government should involve itself directly in this topic, which is primarily a matter for private enterprise. Indeed, the Government believes the best way it can help any sector of business flourish is not by intervening, but by providing a general economic framework which encourages growth and at the same time removing unnecessary restrictions or burdens.
> 3. Yet Government has many interests in tourism and leisure. It is itself in the business, through ownership of national museums and galleries, the preservation of ancient buildings and monuments, support for the arts, sport and recreation, and the conservation of the countryside. It is involved in the way people get to and around this country – airports, seaports, railways, roads, waterways. Government Departments set many of the rules which regulate the industry, such as liquor licensing, shop hours, advertising restrictions, and employment legislation. Government gives grant aid to the statutory Tourist Boards, which provide marketing and advisory services to the industry, and through the Boards to a range of tourism development projects.
> 4. Finally, the government has a direct concern with the industry's great potential for growth, job creation and enterprise. As patterns in society and industry change, we need to encourage the new strong points of our economy, many of them in service sectors. Across the UK few industries offer as great a scope for new employment as tourism and leisure, much of it in self-employment or small firms, involving a far wider range of skills than most other growth sectors and a broad geographical spread.
> 5. That is above all why the government has taken a fresh look at whether there are obstacles it can remove in order to enable this important sector of industry to develop further and faster. Two main areas of improvement have been studied – ways in which business can be made easier for the industry itself; and ways in which people can get more out of their time off, which in turn must benefit business too[3].

In turn the British Tourist Authority publishes from time to time a Strategy Document which concentrated more specifically as an operating agency of Government on implementing policy particularly through its international marketing operations.

The latest report *Strategy for Growth* (BTA 1989)[4] sets out the following objectives for the British Tourist Authority (BTA) which is the British Tourism Agency for Government.

Statutory Responsibilities and Objectives of BTA

Statutory Responsibilities

The British Tourist Authority was, in common with the English, Scottish and Wales Tourist Boards, established under the Development of Tourism Act 1969. The Authority assumed the principal responsibilities of the British Travel Association which until then had been Britain's national tourist organisation.

The BTA's responsibilities are to:

a) promote tourism to Britain from overseas;
b) advise Government on tourism matters affecting Britain as a whole;
c) encourage the provision and improvement of tourist amenities and facilities in Britain.

The National Tourist Boards' responsibilities are to:

a) promote their own country as a tourist destination
b) encourage the provision and improvement of tourist facilities and amenities within their own country

BTA Objectives

1. To maximise the benefit to the economy of tourism to Britain from abroad, while working worldwide in partnership with the private and public sector organisations involved in the industry and the English (ETB), Scottish and Wales Tourist Boards.
2. To identify the requirements of visitors to Britain, whatever their origin, and to stimulate the improvement of the quality of product and the use of technology to meet them.
3. To spread the economic benefits of tourism to Britain more widely and particularly to areas with tourism potential and higher than average levels of unemployment.
4. To encourage tourism to Britain in off-peak periods.
5. To advise Government on tourism matters affecting Britain as a whole.
6. To ensure that the Authority makes the most cost-effective use of resources in pursuing its objectives.

The Department of Employment for the UK published an Annual Report on its Tourism Activities *Action for Jobs in Tourism*[5] in 1986 and described Government's role in Tourism as follows:

The Government's role
While the development of the UK tourism and leisure industries must be mainly the responsibility of the private sector working as appropriate with local authorities, central government's involvement, as indicated in *Pleasure, Leisure and Jobs*, is significant. The Government will continue:

– to deal with administrative or other obstacles which stand in the way of the industry's development
– to identify ways in which Government programmes can give greater support to tourism's contribution towards employment generation.

The Government will also continue to give full weight to the growing economic importance of this industrial sector in their own spending plans. Expenditure on support for tourism and tourism projects, on conserving the countryside and the natural environment, maintaining the heritage and encouraging sport, was £Sterling 320 million in 1985/86.

Spreading the benefit

New focus

The Government's key objectives are to spread the economic and employment benefits of tourism more widely around the country and to encourage tourism activity outside the main holiday season. This is why new guidance, and additional resources, have been provided to the BTA and the ETB in the current year.
They have been asked to give particular attention – in both marketing and development programmes – to encouraging tourism in areas of the country with untapped tourism potential and higher than average levels of unemployment, and to extending the tourism season.
To this end the provision for their grants-in-aid and for Section 4 support has been increased by 20 per cent to Sterling 6 million for 1986/87, giving a combined total of Sterling 40 million. Much of this expenditure is being directed at new initiatives. For example:

– the BTA is marketing the year-round attractions of Britain to young people in Japan and Hong Kong and designing new campaigns in Europe to feature the northern and western parts of Britain.
– the ETB is mounting a major campaign with the four northern regional tourist boards to promote England's North Country in London and the South East; a new cities campaign highlighting the tourism potential of inner city areas; and a new off-season promotion featuring the West Country and the Heart of England.

A recent official examination of tourism in Spain[6] is instructive in reporting on the respective public and private sector roles. 'The overriding final cause of the tourism recession was summed up as the loss of value for money in the product offered.' The main reasons behind this loss of value for money were divided into those for which the state should take full responsibility, those which were due to deficiencies in both the public and private sectors, and those which could be attributed solely to the private sector, as follows:

Public sector:
Spanish roads and traffic conditions (inferior)
Railway transport (not suited to mass transport)
Air transport (air traffic control delays etc)
Sea transport
Post and telecommunications (described as chaotic)
Hygiene, environment, noise, ecology, and beach cleanliness
Other factors criticised as hindering development:
Urban security
Taxes
Lack of coordination, central and regional government
Lack of clear legal framework for certain activities (eg time share)

Public and private sectors:
Exchange rate
Service and training
Complementary facilities (activities in addition to accommodation and climate)

Private sector responsibility:
Quality of product
Marketing
Traditional standards for hospitality for foreign visitors diminishing.

Government tourism functions

The principal departments of the Government will have functions affecting the travel trade. In Brussels at least ten out of the 23 Directorates of the Commission of the European Communities have tourism responsibilities, usually more far reaching than that of the one Directorate (DG XXIII) nominally responsible for tourism matters. The following Governmental activity can control the basic conditions for tourism development:

1. Financial and fiscal regulation (including customs and excise);
2. Transport policy, and in certain cases transport operation eg state railways, road building and transport infrastructure; security and policing: including frontier controls, passports, visas etc;
3. Health and social services;

4. Environment and conservation, including planning controls.

Major tourist attractions will be directly affected by the government agencies responsible eg heritage and cultural activity is generally an area for state intervention. So also is sport and recreation. The provision of recreation infrastructure may be very costly and *unprofitable*. Many of these functions may be devolved not only to specialist agencies but to local (and regional) government.

Trade and commerce

A wide range of regulation and encouragement is a common governmental task, and may cover the principal industries or economic sectors. Tourism may be left out or treated as low priority. Financial incentives for development of industry should be available for tourism as well as manufacturing trades. In many cases tourism may contribute more effectively to the implementation of government policies, for example the regeneration of declining urban or rural areas. It is common practice for local government to subvent or operate tourist facilities in the cultural and recreation field, basically for their own residents. However in resorts investment is made for visitors, where they are recognised as the principal trade of the locality. Local government has invested massively in recent years in conference halls, exhibition centres, theatres and leisure attractions, transport and visitor infrastructure. In some cases local authorities develop sea ports and airports directly or in joint schemes with the private sector, and have a key role in road and parking provision.

The recent expansion in urban and city short stay visits throughout the year: city tourism for cultural, sporting, and entertainment attractions including shopping provides a new source of prosperity which is changing attitudes in many commercial and industrial centres. Glasgow, for example was proclaimed the European City of Culture in 1990.

Municipal leadership and action to enhance basic destination attractions is vital. The private sector cannot undertake such functions and cannot operate unless they are performed adequately. There is a wide field for joint public/private sector co-operation but this must follow the formulation and acceptance of policy and strategy, the provision of basic infrastructure and establishing a system of consultation and co-ordination linking the public and private sector areas of action. Typically in a resort the resort authority will provide this focal point, but there may be an efficient joint agency such as the *syndicat d'initiative* in France stimulating the co-operative as opposed to the competitive tasks of trade.

Thus the principal departments of state have an important tourism role whether they recognise it or not. Furthermore for efficient and successful development of tourism as a major industry contributing substantially to national prosperity co-ordination within the government machine and in its liaison with the operating private sectors is essential. This is all the more necessary as government is usually a major operator and investor in travel services, recreation and cultural services. It is also the principal beneficiary in tourism spending, as unlike the export of physical goods, tourist transactions are regarded as domestic trade and fully taxed. It has been estimated that in the UK tourists contribute over Sterling 1 billion per year directly to government through such taxes as VAT (Value Added Tax) and excise duties on liquor, tobacco and petrol. This is an amount far in excess of any direct investment by the state in tourism services including work of the State Tourist Organisation. The situation is similar in many other countries in Western Europe. Governments' tourism administration is not always satisfactory. The trade requires professional skills which the state administrators lack.

Tourism is now a major economic and social force. According to the World Tourism Organisation it will shortly become, if it has not already done so, the largest single trade in the world. The Commissioner for Tourism of the European Community claimed that it was the largest single trade in the community at the opening of the European Year of Tourism 1990. Most governments have recognised a public interest by establishing a department and an agency eg a national tourist board, to deal with the subject. This may take many forms but its first responsibility must be to ensure an effective system of co-ordination and co-operation between the departments of state intervening in travel business and working with the private sector. Unfortunately the results are often far from satisfactory. Priority and resources given to tourism are usually low and co-ordination is weak, limiting the successful development at both national and international levels.

The principal tourism functions of the State can be summarised briefly:

1. Formulating policy and approving broad strategy for development;
2. Regulation and inspection including consumer protection;
3. Provision of a consultative forum as a basis for co-operation and co-ordination: the range of tourism interest is so wide that this is an essential function;
4. Intervention if required in the fiscal area, and financial assistance for development of infrastructure and other investment;

5. Establishing favourable conditions for private sector operation;
6. Information, statistics and research, including market research;
7. Promotion for the destination overseas;
8. Operations in the case of market failure where the private sector cannot initiate or develop some essential service. It is for example common practice at local level for the public sector to invest in conference and exhibition facilities, and in a wide range of cultural, sporting and recreational facilities.

Government may devolve operating functions to the local level or to specialist agencies. The Organisation for Economic Co-operation and Development (OECD) published a farsighted account of the state's national task in 1960[1]. It is normal for a State Tourist Office or National Tourist Board to handle marketing and the provision of visitor reception services. It may also ensure liaison with the private sector and operate in partnership with the trade, thus greatly increasing efficiency. In Europe the National Tourist Offices for the Northern countries – Britain, the Scandinavian countries, The Netherlands, Germany, Ireland, Switzerland and Austria – have state agencies for promotion separate from the Government Tourist Department and operate jointly with the private sector to a greater or lesser degree. In the case of the British Tourist Authority about two thirds of its marketing spend overseas comes from joint schemes with industry and tourism operating interests.

The State's intervention in infrastructure and tourism plant is often delegated to a specialist agency. In many cases this is not the State Tourist Office. It may be a regional development board, for example the Scottish Development Agency now Scottish Enterprise and the Highlands and Islands Development Board in Scotland now the Highlands and Islands Enterprise; and the agencies set up in the *new towns* in Britain, such as the London Docklands Development Corporation, a state body specifically designed for the purpose.

Furthermore there has to be a whole plan for major tourism development. Private enterprise may contribute many pieces of the jigsaw, but there must be a complete picture, a co-ordinated action to create the destination and its unique or competitive attractions to appeal to the chosen clientele. Tourism is theatrical. There will be many shows, but there has to be a director to get the *act* together. The initiative of action may come from commerce. The London Tourist Board was created in 1960 on the initiative of Lord Forte the founder of Trusthouse Forte, one of the largest hotel and catering companies in the world, and a group of travel service operators. But it required the agreement and support of the London local Government, and assistance from the National Tourist Organisation to realise the objectives and programmes.

Figure 10.2 Division of responsibility in the development of Languedoc – Rousillon, France

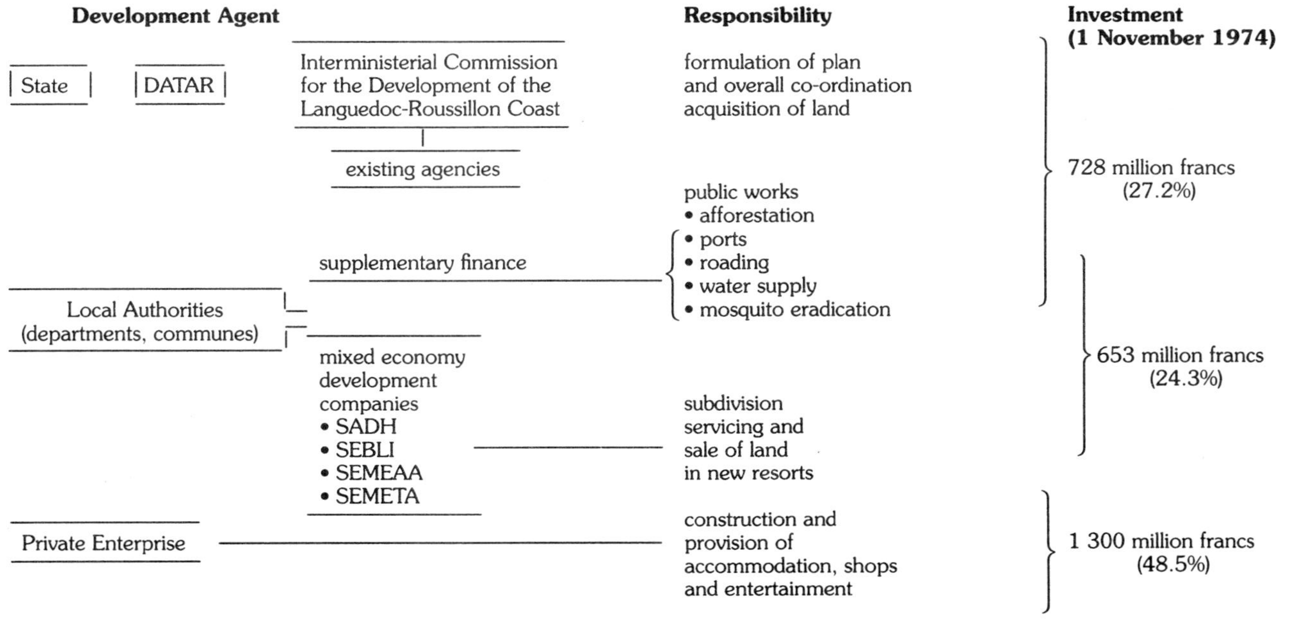

Tourism plans

Professor Douglas Pearce in his book *Tourist Development*[2] gives a useful account of major schemes in France: Languedoc-Roussillon, the French Alps; Cancun in Mexico; and Spain. The examples show how the central and local government establish the necessary machinery for public/private sector co-operative action to create the resort area, and the different effects of varying tourism policies and degrees of control. Where the state has acted remotely, and the resort planning left largely to private developers, as in Spain, the results have not always been satisfactory.

France Languedoc-Roussillon

The State was firstly responsible for drawing up the overall development plan. Following this plan it oversaw and controlled all subsequent phases of the operation through a small but important study team. Secondly, as was noted above, the State acquired all the necessary land for the operation to go ahead as planned. Thirdly, it was responsible for undertaking major infrastructural works; the road networks, the ports, afforestation, water supply and much of the mosquito eradication. Finally, State finance was made available to the other authorities to undertake their responsibilities.

Administrative innovations facilitated the work of the State. In 1963 a *Mission Interministerialle* was created under DATAT *(Delegation a l'Amenagement du Territoire et a l'Action Regionale)*, drawing together representatives of the interested government ministeries (finance, interior, development, agriculture and tourism). The Mission was a surprisingly small organization, much of its work being the responsibility of a small study team, consisting of a dozen people. Their role was very much a co-ordinating one, many of the initial studies and most of the actual development work being undertaken by the appropriate government department to which it transferred the necessary finance from the Mission's central budget.

Vars

The catalytic effect of the intervention of a large outside company is clearly evident at Vars (*Hautes Alpes*). Although the commune's potential as a major ski-resort was recognised before the Second World War, the few hundred Varsins, for the most part small farmers, lacked the means to develop more than four or five simple lifts and a few small hotels and chalets in the immediate post-war period. With local agricultural in decline, the commune was stagnating and suffering steady population losses through out-migration. This situation changed in 1958, with the election of a new mayor, a former politician from Paris. The new mayor was able to interest a group of Paris-based financial concerns in forming a company, the (*Société pour l'Equipement et le Developpement de Vars*) SEDEV, to develop Vars as a tourist resort. Unlike the local population, the SEDEV had both the financial and technical resources to create a network of lifts large enough to launch the resort on a national scale. As the SEDEV constructs each stage of the network the commune, in the terms of a formal contract, cedes a specified area of land to the company for the development of accommodation.

Cancun, Mexico

Similarly in the new Mexican complex of Cancun created *ex nihilo* on the Caribbean coast of Quintana Roo, almost half of the $47 million public investment in the first phase of development was financed by a loan from the Inter-American Development Bank. A further loan of $20 million in 1976 accounted for a similar proportion of the second stage of development (Cazes, 1980b).

Development of Cancun is the responsibility of FONATUR (*Fondo Nacional de Fomento de Turismo*), a central government agency whose aim is 'to achieve a controlled increase in tourism by improvement and expansion of existing resorts and the creation of new tourist zones focused on newly created cities' (Collins, 1979, p. 353). FONATUR has been responsible for the selection of the site (after an intensive nationwide inventory of sites and resources), acquisition of the land, preparation of the plan, development of the infrastructure and servicing of the site prior to its sale to the private sector. FONATUR has also participated jointly in the actual development of various hotels but that has been left mainly to the private sector, with 80 per cent of the private investment estimated to be Mexican in origin.

Spain

Development of the coast south of Alicante to Cabo de Palos is more recent than that part of the Costa Blanca to the north. Development there has taken the form of a series of *large Centros de Interes Turistico Nacional* (CITN), resort enclaves in which the activities of the tour operators have been linked with those of real estate promoters. As CITNs, these developments benefit from generous credit facilities and fiscal assistance from the State (*Vila Fradera*, 1966). With the exception of Santa Pola del Este which has been grafted on to a fishing port with some established holiday homes, the others – La Zenia, Dehesa de Campoamor and Lan Manga del Mar Menor – have been developed *ex nihilo* on large agricultural holdings at the initiative of the land owner.

> Torres Bernier (1985) points to the new division of responsibilities which have resulted form the creation of autonomous regions in Spain during the early 1980s. Central government is left with the role of promoting tourism abroad, managing pre-existing facilities such as the chain of Paradores Nacionales as well as with more general policies affecting tourism, such as those of economic stabilisation. The autonomous regional governments, such as those for Catalonia and Andalucia, now have responsibility for the development and planning of tourism plant, domestic tourism and related areas of interest, for example the environment, regional planning and leisure and recreation. While the full impact of these changes has yet to be seen, Torres Bernier suggests the relatively indiscriminate development of accommodation under national policies dominated by balance of payments considerations may no longer be tolerated by the regions.

This illustrates again the importance of the Tourism Policy and Plan, and the consultation and co-ordination process leading to agreement and understanding between the interests. The OECD has charted changes in government tourism policies in recent years. The immediate post war years concentrated on the national benefits from foreign currency earnings and improvements in the balance of payments. Unrestricted expansion in volume as well as value lead to revision as countries became wealthier. Mass tourism's disadvantages in congestion, cultural and social confiict, environmental damage etc resulted in a more sophisticated approach. Governments became more interested in tourism as a means of regional development especially to bring prosperity to poorer rural areas with little industrialisation. Later still tourism's value as a creator of jobs, and the right kind of jobs in particular was selected as the mainspring of policy and government intervention.

These changes have important repercussions on tourism growth and thus on development schemes. In 1974 for example the Government in the UK issued new Tourism Guidelines seeking to redistribute tourism fiows to the poorer regions, or places where industrial dereliction made new sources of prosperity essential. Tourists were to be redirected away from London for this purpose, an example of mistaken administration, because that is where the tourist wanted to go, and the market is in control. It was essential in a competitive situation to persuade visitors first of all to come to the UK through the London gateway before they could be encouraged to visit the regions.

Effectively much sensible tourism planning is held up or handicapped by policy mistakes, confusion and lack of accepted leadership. The government role is crucial. No one else can represent the whole community which is inevitably involved in large scale modern tourist development. Government must decide policy, set the necessary rules, and accept public responsibility for fair conditions of trade, welcome and hospitality.

Potential national cost and benefits are enormous. To adopt a policy of *laissez-faire* and leave action to the operating or private sector can only result in a lopsided travel movement with investment conditioned by short term considerations where profit alone determines the action. Many aspects of tourism cannot be handled on a free market basis. Apart from *market failures* and error, there are many infrastructure prerequisites which either cannot be profitable on their own account or are unsuited to private sector operation for example in public transport, cultural and recreational activity, and health and safety provision.

Some of the results in Britain of the retreat of government from such intervention are far from promising for the future. The Channel Tunnel rail link, airport and air traffic control congestion, limitations generally on investment in transport infrastructure do not provide a good basis for the anticipated expansion in international travel nor do they compare well with action taken by some European competitors. The open door policy invites foreign carriers to take over British companies and routes whether charter companies or shipping services for example the sale of the national carrier *Sealink* to foreign owners.

Britain's tourism balance of payments is in the red to the extent of £3 billion and the transport balance, the excess of payments to foreign sea and air carriers compared with foreign spending on British ships and planes, is well over £1 billion. Yet until the 1980s there was a substantial annual credit balance. European governments are active in investment protection and operations in these fields.

The British exhibition industry has only 25 per cent of the international exhibition space offered by France or Germany. Yet trade fairs are the market place of modern industry. The 1992 Single Market will make competition in Europe a key factor. London and the South East, the highway to and from Europe needs a major modern Trade Fair Centre comparable to the National Exhibition Centre (NEC) in Birmingham and able to compete with European cities' facilities. But even if a suitable site could be found the cost would exceed £500 million and without public sector support and involvement there is no hope of getting commercial action. All the major centres of the Continent are publicly financed and the public sector promotes and organises fairs. In Britain this is left largely to private enterprise. The hard attitude to local government initiatives and investment makes it more difficult for the British resorts to regenerate themselves.

The French government recently with massive financial support helped to establish Disney World near Paris as a major European visitor attraction. The Disney Company looked at a number of alternatives including London but were discouraged by the lack of any state support in the UK. The loss of traffic to the UK from this one investment will be large and continue for many years. No new resort has been built in Britain since the Aviemore scheme in Scotland in 1960. Although on a small scale, substantial state support was required for the realisation of the plan. There is nothing surprising in this. It is common practice for the state to create industries, industrial centres, attract major foreign investment (motor car factories), build up airlines and other transport companies and finance major schemes such as garden festivals, which need major infrastructure investment. The Local Authority in particular has a special role in initiating tourism plans and projects.

Government tasks

The economic and social importance of tourism and the incidence on the resident community are too great to leave the development of future trade entirely to the private sector. Government has an interest in or must accept responsibility for action in the following fields:

1. International trade and at least the longer term implications of the balance of trade and payments. There must be fair competition. National or international industries – some publicly owned – must enjoy favourable conditions for prosperous trading and investment.
2. Government is vitally concerned with employment and training. Tourism is the largest single employer, and offers greater opportunities for new job creation through future expansion than any other industry.
3. Tourism is an effective agency for regional development, urban regeneration and redistribution of income and prosperity between richer and poorer areas.
4. Tourism is a natural partner for agriculture and a suitable development in rural regions which can help to stabilise resident populations and provide the necessary infrastructure of transport and public services needed for secondary industry and commercial growth. The EC has recognised the importance of tourism in offering alternative economic support in areas where agricultural production is declining or suffering readjustment through changing government policies reflecting new and different needs.

5. The state has always accepted rural responsibilities. Government may have social policies for recreation, health, education and other services involving travel: youth, senior citizens, disabled etc.

Stages of growth

The roles of the public and private sectors, always in partnership implicit or explicit, will vary greatly from time to time, depending on the stage of tourism expansion and the political *will* which should be reflected in a published tourism plan. This is always essential if the private sector comprising many different services and small businesses is to contribute to a cohesive and effective total destination appeal.

There are three stages in the Destination's Life Cycle:

1. Exploration, Experimenting and Initiation
This will involve the public authority, national or local, but may be led by a single entrepreneur from the public or private sectors. In developing countries the government must take the lead. Plans will be tentative and easily changed and marketing has a key role to play in a process of trial and error.
2. Main period of growth sometimes referred to as take off. The private sector will tend to move into a dominating position, but the public authority through planning and infrastructure control must remain in charge of the longer term strategy. As expansion and investment involves major commitments it will become increasingly difficult to change the main course of growth, thus the original longer term plans will have important repercussions.
3. The third stage is that of maturity which in turn may lead to stagnation, slow growth or decline and eventually depending on community action destruction or regeneration. The last stage represents the reaction to longer term market trends and their influence on the destinations trade after it reaches maturity. The whole process from *birth* to *decline* traditionally took many years indeed even centuries.

But the speed of change has greatly increased in demand trends, and often on a massive scale. Furthermore, techniques of investing and building, plant, equipment and infrastructure has similarly been transformed. Development is now rapid, London's total good standard hotel stock (rooms with bath) doubled in four years 1970–74 as a result of government intervention, when 30,000 rooms with bath were constructed on a subsidised basis. Building and investments are no longer undertaken for use by generations, but for a relatively short life. They are from the technical point of view not difficult to renew. Sadly planners and entrepreneurs, with their extended powers and scale of operation have made grave mistakes destroying irreplaceable heritage treasures to make way for easily replaceable substitutes which may have little lasting value.

Levels of activity

Almost all cities and towns and indeed many rural areas, at least in industrialised countries are visitor destinations. There cannot be any that are unvisited or totally isolated. But there are different levels of activity just as there are differing stages of growth.

Three main levels of activity predominate. Firstly all destinations will enjoy a degree of communication travel, for business, family or social reasons. Many will encourage travel: for example for business, conferences and events to stimulate the local trade. This form of travel can by modest encouragement represent tourism at its most profitable stage, using specialist appeals (trade or education) to *sell* the surplus of reception and transport services unused by the local residents. Centres should strive very hard for this type of profitable business which offers great community benefits, but total traffic and revenues may remain modest. Initiatives may come from a commercial co-operative – a tourist promotion association, but some support and a degree of encouragement and leadership will be required from the local authority if the trade is to grow beyond the complementary *fill the empty hotel beds* stage.

At the second level the town or area chooses the travel movement as a major industry but in partnership with existing local activity and the major industries of the place where both sit happily with the natural resources of the locality. The best example is that of tourism and agriculture in rural communities. This has become a major element of policy in the EC, where tourism is seen as an important social as well as economic force to stabilise rural populations and support the necessary modern infrastructure of transport and services ensuring an acceptable quality of life for the residents.

The third level is where the town or area decides to choose tourism – normally this is holiday travel – as its main business. The great resorts have grown up in this way. In recent years the period of expansion has been short with a rapid and sometimes massive build up of visitor infrastructure. Although tourism is regarded as a service industry it is often overlooked in planning that the movement is a major user of expensive long term capital investment in basic plant: transport, accommodation and leisure equipment. The rewards are great, the opportunities seemingly never ending, but there are also great dangers.

Expansion and the enormous demand potential may obscure other key characteristics of change; volatility, diversification, specialisation, and rapid alterations in fashion and trends. There are now a number of *mini-mass markets* differing in their rates of growth, degrees of maturity, and resilience to price or recession. Senior citizen movement for example is relatively stable and capable of growth in a recessed market. Markets can be defined by segments, and need to be compared by careful analysis of product and capacity as a first stage in the planning process. The market not the product dictates the outcome. Misunderstanding of this key aspect can lead to costly error. Sometimes product descriptions are mistaken for *markets*, and some are theoretically described with no relevance to the powers of the market place or the disciplines of profit an loss. For example, coastal tourism, city tourism, offseason tourism, rural tourism, social tourism, marine tourism etc, and recently eco-tourism and soft tourism. These terms may be useful in theories but lack the practical imperatives of the market place and the market segments. Visitors do not buy coast or rural or social tourism but a collection of specific satisfactions at a chosen destination which has its own image and recognised appeal. The packaging process may be an important element with the wholesaler, travel agent, or institution in charge of the shop in the market place.

Planners function

The planning process is fundamental and must be co-ordinated by the public sector. It may be initiated by private developers, or even through Parliament or the local authority. This was certainly the case in the European Community where the interest of the Parliament stimulated an unwilling executive to action in producing a first EC policy for the trade.

Planning is concerned with the management of resources, many of which will be in public ownership or control. Management must have particular objectives for the town, or region or country. But in market economies the consumer and marketing criteria will be paramount and dictate options for action. The consumer in international and national tourism is king.

But the planners in turn must be clear about their own function. Who are they planning for? This will vary according to public and private sector interest. The local authority must have the local residents' interest in mind, but the financial disciplines of local traders and investors will influence options. So too will the intervention of national or in some case supranational government, if there is discrimination in favour of certain kinds of investment, in areas needing economic regeneration for example, or in selection of key sites.

It is at the very early stages of establishing the plan, at whatever level of sophistication and growth, that consultation and partnership between the public and private sector is crucial. They each have their roles to play but they must start by knowing where the goalposts are, and contributing to the structure of the grand design for the future. Furthermore the private sector as much as the public sector will contribute the market knowledge and expertise which will identify options and cost benefits, and monitor progress as the design unfolds. This essential partnership is greatly assisted if there is some form of cooperative tourism organisation such as tourist board with trade links; *syndicat d'initiative*, or marketing agency, and within the public authority tourism decision-taking at a very senior level with professional advice and an effective management team to implement agreed programmes.

References

1 Tourist Development and Economic Growth *OECD Paris 1966*
2 *Professor Douglas Pearce* Tourist Development, *Longman 1989*
3 *Pleasure Leisure and Jobs* HMSO 1985
4 *Strategy for Growth* BTA 1989
5 *Action for Jobs in Tourism* Central Office of Information 1986
6 Economist Intelligence Unit *International Tourism Report No.4. 1990*

Appendix

Extract from Tourist Development and Economic Growth OECD (Paris) 1966

The role of the national tourist organisation

In formulating its tourism policy, a government will have a number of possible options before it. It will have to decide, for example, the appropriate rate of growth it wishes to see in the tourism sector, whether to encourage mass tourism or to cultivate a slower and more selective growth. It will have to determine what should be the respective roles of the public and the private sector in developing the tourist industry, and similarly, of domestic and foreign capital. It must establish the due importance to be given to the needs of the tourism sector in plans for national and regional development and in so doing must make a decision regarding the time-scale that it considers reasonable for planning forward investments in the tourism industry. There is further the question of whether to treat tourism in the same way as any other growth sector or whether the nature of the industry requires special administrative and credit arrangements.

Tourism involves a number of considerations that are non-economic in nature. Tourism often has significant cultural implications (for example, the restoration of ancient monuments); aesthetic (the preservation of beauties of landscape and the safeguarding of the nation's heritage); social (the provision of recreational facilities for the health and welfare of the people); and political (the improvement of international understanding). These considerations, however, are simply a few of the many alternatives among which a government must choose in deciding the objectives for which it intends to allocate its budget. These are primarily social objectives and, as such, they must be costed and the determination of how much of the national resources should be devoted to them is essentially a matter of social policy. The formulation of the government's tourism programme on the other hand should be determined, primarily, by consideration of economic policy, on the basis of the benefits to the economy which may be expected to follow.

These differences of function are reflected in the organisation's structure and constitutional status. Thus in some countries, the national tourism office is a part of the central machinery of government through which the government operates directly in the tourism sector. In others, it has semi-autonomous status and functions not as an organ of government but rather as a professional body outside it. As a general rule, it may be said that this latter conception of the role of the national tourism office is more appropriate to countries where tourism is already fairly advanced and where the private sector is active in it. In countries which are only starting to develop their tourism potential or where it is desired to make a rapid push forward, the government will normally play a more active role itself in promoting tourism development and will use the tourism office as its administrative organ for the purpose.

There is no set formula as to what constitutes the most satisfactory constitutional arrangement for the national tourism body. In some countries, tourism ranks as a full Ministry and in some its Minister enjoys Cabinet rank. Other possibilities include making it semi-autonomous and largely independent of the regular structure of government.

There is clearly a correlation between the standing that the government accords the national tourism organisation and its estimates of the importance of tourism to the national economy, although other considerations, political and psychological, also enter in. Another index of government recognition is the amount of funds that the government makes available to it. In some countries, the activities of the national tourism office are financed in part by means of a direct tax on tourists. As a general rule, however, this is not to be recommended, partly on psychological grounds (it tends to create resentment on the part of the customer) and partly on economic, because through its multiplier effects, tourism is already making a valuable contribution to tax revenue. A special tax on tourists is therefore tantamount to taxing them twice, and, moreover, imposing a surcharge on exports.

At the 1963 General Assembly of the International Union of Official Travel Organisations, it was suggested that the national tourist budget should be not less than one per cent of tourist receipts. This however should not be taken as a rigid formula, since for a country whose tourism development is still in its early stages, its yield would obviously be inadequate.

Whatever the constitutional or financial base, the national tourism office in any country will be the officially recognised expert body on tourism matters. As such, it will have the responsibility of preparing the basic studies and forecasts on which the government can prepare the national tourism programme; it will act as spokesman for the interests of the tourism sector; and will assist either directly or indirectly in the implementation of the government's tourism policy. The interpretation of this latter responsibility will, clearly, depend on the government's conception of its own role in tourism development. Thus the functions of the national tourist office may be solely advisory, or regulatory, or they may also be directly operational and promotional.

The administrative structure and composition of the national tourism body will be geared to the functions that it has to perform. A national tourism office would normally include sections to cover the following functions:

1. Research;
2. Information and promotion within the country;
3. Regularisation of standards of lodgings and restaurants;
4. Control of activities of private travel agencies;
5. Publicity overseas;
6. Technical and juridical problems;
7. International relations;
8. Development of selected tourist areas;
9. Overall tourism policy and promotion.

Even where it has a large degree of operational responsibility, it must decide which things it is going to do itself and which it should properly divide with other agencies of government. It has also to decide to what extent it should call in specialists, as for example, for research and forecasting, or for public relations and publicity campaigns. It may also choose sometimes to work in collaboration with the public or the local authorities, as for example in organising a festival.

Whatever the tasks that the national tourism body is called upon to do, what is essential is that it should have the full powers necessary to carry them out. It must, above all, have authority. It must be able to present effectively the case for tourism among the claims of other sectors competing for government support and finance. In a situation where the imperatives of tourism development impinge on those of other sectors and there is a conflict of interests, as in the location of a highway or the priority to be given to a new airport, the head of the tourism organisation should be listened to with as much respect as the Ministers of Public Works or Aviation.

It is essential also that it be technically competent and recognised as such. The wide range of functions devolving upon it require a high degree of experience and professionalism and the calibre and prestige of the senior management of the national tourism organisation can be important factors in the effectiveness with which the government puts through its tourism policy.

Finally, it is essential that the tourism office recognises the limitations of its own mandate, however that may be defined, and maintains close and harmonious liaison with all the other interests that may be involved in tourism development. Three principal interests are concerned. The first is the national planning organisation. In most countries there is regular provision for this liaison at the national level. On the regional level, however, the situation is often less satisfactory and regional planners, and physical planners in particular, often fail to co-ordinate their work sufficiently with that of the local tourist bodies.

The second is liaison with the other departments of government, partly as a matter of information and negotiation between different interests eg labour regulations, taxation, etc and partly for the infrastructure and services needed for tourism development and which will normally fall to other departments to provide. Thirdly there must be the fullest co-operation with the private sector. This should begin, properly, at the planning stage, when the government should be preparing its programme in consultation with local and private interests. It should continue by means of frequent and informal contacts to ensure harmonious collaboration on the practical problems involved in making the programme into a profitable business.

11 International agencies

International tourism is by its nature essentially dependent on good international communication and cooperation. Thus international organisation has an important value in its development at both public and private sector level. There is a continuing need for exchange of information and expertise between countries and regular contact and co-operation in many fields. It is vital to create conditions for free or liberal international movement of people, and the freedom to trade internationally in travel services. This may seem obvious, but freedom and removal of constraints on free movement of people, services and capital is far from achievement in world travel today .Only government collective action at the international level can bring this about. The principal international agencies concerned have a major role to play in securing the necessary freedoms.

Much progress has been made over the past three decades following complex discussions and multilateral agreements between countries to secure the current level of mass movement. This has resulted from operations of a sophisticated travel retail and wholesale industry backed up by large and powerful trade sectors to service mass traffic.

Although the present state of international co-operation and regulation has permitted substantial and successful growth, the situation is by no means satisfactory, since tourism continues to grow. Governments tend to legislate for the problems and opportunities of yesterday. World travel has doubled in two decades to the present level of over 400 million international visits in 1990. Most experts forecast potential expansion at least as great in the next decade, and the possibility of an accelerated expansion for the principal world travel markets.

International organisations

There are a number of key international organisations concerned with world travel. The wide range of interests involved need focal points, machinery and systems for co-operation and co-ordination at all the main levels of action. This applies particularly to Government and the public sector. Indeed without a substantial degree of multilateral action at the official level there could never be a mass travel movement. The reception staff in international travel, officials and providers, must be user friendly. There has to be a high degree of co-operation and partnership, and its absence a common cause of failure in planning and implementation.

From early days recognition of passports, and measures to facilitate *bona fide* personal travel, even in times of war, was agreed as a necessary role and objective for governments. In many ways current attitudes have got worse rather than better. In past times travel and the traveller were held in high esteem. Travel was a respected activity and practised by the *best* people, educated and relatively prosperous because movement was slow and expensive. Tourism has no such status. It is a downgraded term.

With mass traffic, controls, security and health and safety checks have multiplied. After the last war when personal travel began again, a new system was needed to remove many absolute constraints on travel, for example to restore foreign currency allowances; provide easy access to passports; remove barriers such as visas and exit permits; and major facilitation measures to reduce border delays caused by onerous police and customs controls. The widely practised *Red and Green* customs check required multilateral agreement by governments on customs *allowances* for travellers purchases. The role of international organisations in such facilitation of movement was crucial to success. The Organisation of Economic Co-operation and Development (OECD) and its predecessor the OEEC made a major contribution to the dramatic reduction in border checks delays and travel constraints in its 24 members countries, the richer nations of the world which, account for nearly two thirds of total international traffic. Thus government's role is fundamental in creating conditions for favourable and prosperous development, and in regulating operators of services in the interest of health and safety. More recently action to protect the environment and consumers, and intervention in certain areas of social and labour relations have been politically favoured. There will always be debate about the role of government and the extent of desirable and constructive intervention. Consultation and co-operation with the private sector is essential since most tourist activity requires a degree of public and private sector partnership and co-ordination.

In the case of international tourism Governments must extend their interest to wider areas and in working in partnership with other countries. International organisation and *machinery* is needed for this. Because of its wide ranging nature tourism finds a place in the programmes of a majority of the principal intergovernmental agencies; but in most cases priority given to tourism interests is modest and often minimal. The agencies tend to react to tourism questions and opportunities in the light of their own specialist objectives. There may be little co-ordination of action with other bodies and the results at best disappointing – at worst discouraging or constraining. Recent intervention in Europe by consumer interests have demonstrated the dangers of one sided and unbalanced action.

International agencies' difficulties in dealing with international travel reflect the relatively modest priority given to tourism by a great many national governments, especially in the developed countries. Thus the tourism agency of government which should have an important co-ordinating role is frequently poor in resources and relegated to a junior position in government policy and programmes. The OECD in its latest *Annual Report* on its member governments tourism policy made some significant observations:

> International competition, national interest and the specific features of the tourist industry are all factors that make government intervention in tourism necessary even today. However, the change in emphasis from quantity to quality already presents new challenges for policy-makers.
>
> Policy-making inevitably becomes more complex when qualitative factors have to be taken into account. The value judgements that underpin the final policy choices have to be based on a large number of elements. This requires specialised expertise; the authorities need to be able to call upon such expertise when assessing the overall implications of a phenomenon. In respect of tourism, it was seen that the expertise in government bodies was tending to become more compartmentalised. When this happens, it may become increasingly difficult to ensure that the various parts of a policy are consistent with one another. In some cases, it has been possible to deal with part of the problem by setting up co-ordinating bodies. However, one has the impression that the redistribution of responsibilities that has resulted from the desire for consistency has often been at the expense of those who see things from the specific *tourism* point of view. Governments have to manage a sector that they still do not understand properly. The basis of this understanding must be provided by encouraging pluridisciplinary activity to make the tourism phenomenon clearer. Effective management requires forecasts. Governments therefore need to have longer-term scenarios for future developments in tourism.

The comment is specially significant when OECD member governments are in charge of the developed world which in turn is responsible for the major part of world travel. Yet many government departments and agencies of government are increasingly involved in tourism as the economic and social effects of mass travel become more dominant in many communities. Tourism represents in practice the mobile in contrast to the resident population. Its incidence on the local population at grass roots level as well as at the national level becomes more significant every year.

Intergovernmental agencies must reflect the national situations of their constituents. Many are involved in tourism matters, and some of the technical agencies have major tasks. But they tend to carry out their functions within each one's separate technical *compartments* and without the desirable consultation and co-ordination with the other sectors involved in tourist matters. The result is that an effective tourism policy is inhibited; tourism needs are dealt with piecemeal; and each major issue treated as an offshoot of the principal economic or social policy lines agreed at national or international level. But tourism is an entity in its own right and effective development needs public service treatment and priority accordingly. This needs to be stressed in development plans at national level.

There has been progress over the years. Most major technical arms of government dealing with economic and social subjects recognise the incidence of tourism and give some attention to it. The major United Nations (UN) organs and agencies deal with tourism from time to time, The United Nations Economic and Social Council, The United Nations Conference on Trade and Development (UNCTAD), International Civil Aviation Organisation (ICAO), The World Health Organisation (WHO), International Labour Organisation (ILO), United Nations Education, Scientific and Cultural Organisation (UNESCO), have all been involved to some extent. The World Bank has operated aid programmes for developing countries, but this is not a continuous activity. The UN recognises the World Tourism Organisation (WTO), an intergovernmental agency, as their expert consultative body for the work of government tourism agencies. The WTO carries out training consultative and technical aid programmes with UN support and financial resources, through the United Nations Development Programme (UNDP).

The World Tourism Organisation

Over the years the WTO, and its predecessor body the International Union of Official Tourism Organisations (IUOTO), have a number of successful programmes to their credit. However the work of official international agencies tends to suffer from the one sided nature of government controlled bodies which concentrate on political rather than practical aspects. Errors are compounded because they rarely provide adequate machinery for consultation and co-operation over the range of official services concerned with tourism, and with the operating and private sectors. Working in separate compartments and through closed rather than open administration causes many problems and setbacks. But it is possible to stimulate collection action in the broader aspects of long term planning, and in the crucial areas of policy and strategy. The operating sectors own international agencies have an important role to play in this.

The WTO accepts affiliate members from related tourism interests and commerce, but meetings are infrequent, and the part played by the affiliates in the organisation activities is very limited. They could, if properly organised, provide a *Parliament of Tourism* which would greatly improve technical liaison and co-operation between government and the operating sectors. This is essential for successful development programmes as so many aspects need a partnership approach. The principle has been discussed and there is a greater willingness to move in this direction.

In spite of these shortcomings much progress has been achieved by international agencies in recent years facilitating travel expansion, and providing a forum for consultation, in the exchange of ideas at the official level, collecting and publishing essential information including statistics, organising technical seminars on such vital topics as forecasting, information systems and in training. In this age of communication and technology, an international industry information service is especially important. But it must be operating sector as well as public administration orientated. This is often a weakness.

International tourism needs a growing use of technology at an international level of sophistication and competence. Exchange of information, appraisals of effectiveness of government programmes, methodologies in public administration devoted to tourism, technical aid to developing countries, are all proper functions for an international agency like the WTO, and responsible at the official level for stimulating intergovernmental co-operation and liaison.

These tasks are all the more essential because in most countries the official tourist authority and related agencies (Ministry of Tourism, State Tourist Board or National Tourist Office) are monopolies: only one in each country. They need benchmarks, the comparative checks. They operate in a market dominated world, and usually have some private sector related activity such as international marketing. Thus systems of appraisal, comparative studies and liaison at the industrial level with operating sectors are essential to ensure effective action. Failure can be very costly, yet the price of co-operation through international agencies is relatively inexpensive.

In reality international tourist organisations need and deserve more support than they get from government. Their contribution if well managed can be considerable for modest cost, and much of that due to the relatively high price of international communication. Modern technology however offers very considerable scope for improved efficiency. Governments sometimes resist supporting this form of partnership but are wasteful in inept national administration in tourism, and poorly directed expensive promotion activity. Greater co-operation with the industry in marketing and more professional appraisal and consultation could prove very rewarding.

The WTO publishes at regular intervals reliable technical information and statistics such as: *Current Travel and Tourism Indicators WTO 1990*; and *Yearbook of Tourism Statistics* Vol I Vol II (1988 and annual)[1] WTO.

The statistics showing tourist arrivals and departures by country and season, travel expenditures and receipts, accommodation and transport information with socio-economic data and market segment studies are the basis for the preparation of tourist policies, development strategies and marketing plans. Development plans must be firmly market orientated, as the market will dictate the long term outcome. Although statistical systems may vary and have inherent deficiencies, the figures can still provide the basic information necessary for broad planning, and a base for the use of supplementary information to construct effective programmes in marketing and development work. Basic statistics are vital in development work. A short description of systems, definitions and methodology is included in the appendix to this chapter.

Many of the WTOs technical services and published information are available to all recognised institutions and organisations. Full membership is restricted to governments which inevitably limits the scope for action and practical direction. Liaison with other intergovernmental agencies can produce useful results especially in information services, although co-operation between international agencies tends to be too limited. Lists of qualified consultants are maintained by the WTO and a programme of technical assistance directed to the developing countries is carried out with assistance and financial support from the UNDP.

United Nations agencies and institutions contributing to tourism development activity in past years including the following:

The United Nations Statistical Commission which prepared the internationally accepted definitions and advised on methodology used currently in international travel measurement.
The Economic and Social Council which prepared the first intergovernmental conference on tourism in 1963 leading to substantial progress in facilitation and co-operation.
The International Civil Aviation Organisation (ICAO) responsible for official international action in aviation, covering safety, technical standards and statistics.
The World Health Organisation has been active in health regulation and provisions in international travel.
The International Labour Organisation has done much to encourage training and good labour relations. International travel management and operation needs highly skilled staff. The recognition of training requirements; the provision of resources; and common criteria leading to accepted standards for international qualifications have progressed in recent years, but have not kept up with the heady pace of mass tourism growth worldwide.

Intergovernmental agencies at worldwide level have a useful role to play, notably in setting international standards, information and data bank services including statistics and training. But there are many fields for necessary co-operation best deal with at the regional level, because of geographic ties, or the scale, scope and sophistication of mass trades. Furthermore, many activities should be left properly to the national and competitive interests. There should not be competition between international and national agencies but rather a logical division of tasks, the criterion being what can only be done or best be done at the international co-operative level rather than in the more competitive national sphere.

Regional organisations

When a large enough community of interest exists, for example in the transport trade, some form of tourism liaison machinery will be useful if not essential for successful development. The pace of change and the scale of development in the wealthier countries is such that scope for government action and the responsibilities of the trading sectors are quite different from those in the developing countries. For most of these there will be limited international movement, often needing specialist attention unique to the country concerned. Accordingly the industrialised countries need their own forms of collective co-operation which in certain cases will be a partnership of private and public interests. As an example of this the OECD groups together the 24 rich nations of the world: North America, Western Europe, Australia and Japan. They account for 63 per cent of world tourist arrivals, 72 per cent of tourist receipts and 76 per cent of world travel expenditure. Thus they dominate the world travel scene. They are also the main source of investment resources, expertise and funds for future international growth.

The Tourism Committee of the OECD has a long history of successful multinational action, notably in facilitation. Mass movement across frontiers and land borders between neighbouring countries in particular can no longer be physically controlled on an individual or bespoke system. Indeed the twelve European Community (EC) member countries are planning total abolition of cross border checks with the introduction of the Single Market in 1992. EC governments have pledged to work together to ensure from that time free movement of people, goods and capital. Already checks are perfunctory or on a light sample basis in many of the OECD countries. There are in practice few if any remaining restrictions on personal travel (passports, visas, currency restrictions) and continuing liberalisation in trading except for air transport. This provides the basis for competitive action and the growth of large international companies and chains with benefits as well as problems.

The OECD with the help of its tourism committee publishes a valuable annual report *Tourism Policy and International Tourism*[2] giving detailed information on trends, governments' policy changes, tourist volumes and values (expenditures), and from time to time useful information on specific topics such as accommodation employment and transport. In fact the reports provide an essential basis for development studies in the public and private sector. Governments rarely appraise their policies and strategies publicly and effectively. Yet the need for such action and comparative studies on a professional and technical basis is paramount since a vast trade and a number of great industries are involved as well as a movement of people. Reviews of strategies and change especially in response to market trends and new techniques are as essential for effective government action as for commercial business. The discipline of profits and loss compels companies to appraise their results but governments tend to dodge this key issue.

OECD's tourism work is limited by serious lack of resources allocated to the tourism programme and accordingly poor co-operation with other international agencies and the training sector in general. Government officials change their job frequently yet their responsibilities in the travel trades require a high degree of professionalism and expertise. This together with the relatively low priority accorded to the task is a symptom of a general weakness in the public sector attitude to the trade in many industrialised countries.

The European Community whose twelve member countries account for 45 per cent of Europe's tourism revenues is becoming profoundly important for world tourist development. The EC tourism programme, stimulated by the interest of the European Parliament, is a comparatively recent initiative. A detailed policy statement was first issued in 1986. The reasons given for this new courses of action embracing economic and political aims are instructive[3].

- Economic importance
- Role in the expansion of employment
- Potential for greater understanding and mutual acquaintance
- Advantage to the Community in maintaining its competitive position in international markets.

The proposals for a tourism programme had the following objectives:

- To facilitate tourism in the Community.
- To improve its seasonal and geographic distribution.
- To make better use of Community financial instruments.
- To provide better information and protection for tourists.
- To improve the working conditions of persons employed in the tourism industry.
- To provide more complete information on the sector and set up consultation and co-ordination between the Commission and member states.

The result was an *ad hoc* and piecemeal approach with a very limited budget and programme of activity, with little attempt to fit tourism into the major policies of the Community, which is still not treated as an entity in its own right. Co-ordination of the wide range of activities affecting travel carried out by the various directorates and services has still to be achieved. To be fair to the European Commission the position is no different in many national governments who find the wide ranging nature of the trade difficult to embrace in coherent and collective action by the separate offices of state concerned. Yet unless this happens large scale development of infrastructure and plant as a necessary co-ordinated whole is impossible to achieve.

There are many other official international agencies concerned with travel, for example International Marine Consultative Organisation (IMCO) and the World Bank which from time to time operates a funding operation for government programmes in developing countries, United Nations Conference on Trade and Development (Unctad), United Nations Education, Scientific and Cultural Organisation (UNESCO), and the Council of Europe. Liaison between the agencies is not always effective, and more could be done to exchange information and to consult with specialist organisations both in the public and private sectors. Some of the programmes affecting the trade are not planned with tourism development in mind. There may be cultural objectives and conservation and environmental concerns. Some programmes take a negative view of tourism which can lead to misunderstanding and set back both the specific agency's plans and tourist development. Problems arising from congestion, pressure on fragile areas and resources including historic and natural sites, environmental and cultural clash in developing countries highlight areas needing specialist and professional treatment not intemperate criticism, which can reduce the undoubted potential economic and social benefits from properly organised travel flows.

Non-government agencies

Non-government international agencies are numerous. Some are worldwide in scope – others regional. Two important regional bodies with government agency membership and industry links are the European Travel Commission (ETC) grouping 23 Western European countries and Hungary, and The Pacific Area Travel Association (PATA) with government tourist office members as well as trade constituents. Most Pacific Coast countries including USA, Canada, Australia and Japan are members. These regional bodies are principally concerned with marketing and market research promoting their destination in other continents and regions of the world. They also offer a valuable forum for exchange of information, representation to government and other international interests on matters of prime mutual concern, and encouraging public private sector partnership where this is necessary.

International associations principally concerned with tourism represent the following sectors:

Accommodation: International Hotel Association (IHA)
Transport: International Air Transport Association (IATA), International Union of Railways (UK), International Road Transport Union (UK)
Travel trade: Universal Federation of Travel Agents (UFTA)

Commerce/local government: IULA, ICC
Special interests: ICOMOS, IFCO, IYHA

There are regional associations in the same field such as HOTREC, ECTAA, AEA, EFCT, and *Eurochambres*. With the expansion of the EC tourism programmes there will certainly be a growth of Europe based sector organisations. The principal bodies support the ETAG (European Tourism Action Group) founded by the ETC to stimulate public–private sector partnership. The group has been able to represent the collective tourism view, thus supplementing and supporting the individual sectors work in a valuable way, identifying the common ground in government action, and setting the scene for growth, notably in regard to infrastructure.

Intergovernmental relations are an important part of the work of international trade associations. They can contribute substantially in information gathering, statistics, exchange of technical information through seminars, study groups and research reports. Standard setting and training are common areas of activity. Much of this work can be helpful to developers, especially when the organisations members are traders themselves rather than the national representative body for example IATA, IHA, AIT (World Touring Alliance), and FIA (International Automobile Federation). Virtually all the trading services are represented through international agencies but some are relatively inactive.

In addition to worldwide international representation there are regional groups which play a useful role, for example covering the Americas, Asia and the Pacific, the Middle East, Africa and Europe. In the latter case as already mentioned ETC and ETAG have been developed as useful organisations in an area where common action is becoming more important than separate national endeavour at least at the official level, both for Pan European co-operation and for the twelve EC countries. From the tourism point of view it is very desirable to plan collective work on a Pan European basis rather than for an isolated EC group. Similarly the regional groups need close collaboration, as world tourism grows, through worldwide international bodies in such matters as facilitation or removal of constraints to free travel, standard setting, information systems, and statistics. Long distance travel worldwide is the fastest growing single market segment, and accordingly a worldwide overview in long term planning and strategies is necessary.

Multinational companies

The important role of multinational companies, or the large businesses operating in many countries, if not worldwide, is clearly demonstrated. There is much argument about their contribution to tourism, and to national prosperity in the countries concerned. An objective and professional appraisal of their role is essential for good management.

Although very large commercial companies are growing in size and number, they account for only a small part of worldwide tourism trade, generally less than 10 per cent and an even smaller proportion in the industrialised countries where small business still predominates. Nevertheless they are expanding as economies of scale help dominate markets, and where expertise and fast changing technologies call for massive investment and risk taking. The speed of change also favours large units, as does an increasing conformity in market trends and fashions within major segments. They can create resources quickly, and are better able to respond to rapid change in the market place itself.

The Single EC Market 1992 will undoubtedly encourage the creation of large groups but they are likely to operate worldwide and not confine their operations to the twelve member countries. Already large units are increasingly evident in air transport and certain other passenger services such as cruise ships. Where large scale investment is involved rail and public road transport are candidates for growth. Car hire companies where three major companies, Avis, Hertz and Europcar dominate the European market, is another field for competition and expansion. Hotel and catering chains have been advancing rapidly with American French and British companies leading through Sheraton, Accor, Meridien, THF, Holiday Inns, Hilton.

Trends in hotels and catering company structure have changed significantly in recent times. Growth of the large company chains developed in the USA and spread after the war to Europe with American companies of Hilton and Intercontinental leading the way. Many hotel chains resulted from vertical integration. Railway companies in Britain for example developed hotels with their main city terminal. British Railways had one of the largest chains in Britain until 1980. Airlines needed to guarantee accommodation for their international passengers, all the more so as wide bodied jets stimulated mass long distance and high standard travel. But in the 1980s with more volatile trading conditions, airlines concentrated on their core transport business, and sold hotels to hotel operators (Hilton to the British Ladbroke Company and Intercontinental to Grand Metropolitan, another British company). Thus the current trend is for the multinational hotel companies to concentrate on their accommodation and catering business and not to diversify. They are now expanding worldwide and not simply in Europe, America, or any other single continent.

A major part of the business however may be concentrated in one region or one market segment for example business travel but not exclusively.

Major changes in the travel trade have yet to make themselves felt. There are relatively few large companies most of these are tour operators and virtually all are based on their own large national (domestic) market even when they offer international services over a wider field. Thomas Cook in Britain, American Express in the USA are famous names. They have always had strong international connections but are firmly established in their respective national markets. Both operate large financial services (travellers cheque and/or credit cards) and are more retail travel trade operators than tour organisers. There are signs of major changes in tourism commercial organisations as traffic flows increase.

In spite of tourism's dominance in national economies, particularly in wealthier countries, where it can be responsible for 5 or 10 per cent of GDP, and 5 per cent or more of total jobs, ie. directly employed and doubled that figure if dependent indirect employment is included, the industry remains largely a trade of small businesses and individual personal service. Dr Heeley of the University of Strathclyde estimated that 10 per cent of the two million workers in the UK industry were self employed. Clearly many others are in small firms or indirectly employed. This has some political as well as economic and social advantages not yet fully explored. Large units will grow and increase their share but will never control the trade. There will be special national situations, and in the interest of public benefit and commercial prosperity measures to ensure fair competition in international trading will be essential. This is particularly true for air transport where variations in fares between routes cannot be explained in free market competitive terms.

Generally speaking the march forward of large commercial units operating on a multinational basis in industrialised countries, and especially in Europe must be expected and should be welcomed. This is much needed in the travel trade itself. New multinational institutions or organisations, not necessarily commercial firms responsible for exchanges, health, social groups (eg senior citizens) will grow to meet these new specialist market needs which the traditional tour packaging and retail trade is not servicing.

Criticism of multinational companies has been considerable and at times intemperate in the third world. Yet multinational business can offer substantial benefit to those developing countries starting up the process of creating a successful long term trade. They have expertise, *know-how*, investment funds, managerial competence and most important of all market penetration and control. Indeed for many virgin territories there is no option but to invite such resource owners and managers to help.

But for their part multinational companies are not charities. They are bound by company law, national and international, by the interests and demands of their shareholders, at least in the longer term, and always by the market place, which determines the profits needed for their very existence. Opportunities for investment and for new initiatives in the *developed* world are almost infinite. Furthermore risks may be less and returns more certain.

Accordingly developing countries, with the help of official governmental agencies, must invite and pay for joint scheme partnerships with free enterprise organisations. These countries may be helped by the World Bank, United Nations agencies and other regional governmental groupings for example the EC through their generous Lome Agreement, also national government's technical aid schemes.

Many of the complaints about the activities of foreign investors and operators are theoretical and sometimes illogical. There is a widely held view that such investment leads to *leakage* of scarce foreign currency through capital repayment, cost of foreign labour, and imported materials including food and drink. 'Social and environmental costs or damage are weakening the local culture and life styles': This may be justifiable criticism, and many failings may be due to weakness in management of the countries national tourism resources, inept administration, and errors in development, in the choice of partners, and conditions of joint schemes.

It is the role and duty of the government in the developing world to manage their resources efficiently. This must not be confused with theoretical proposals to manage tourism or visitors. Tourism is basically a movement of people, a demand force and thus a market. It cannot be managed as such. The market will dictate conditions. This false assumption obscures the basic need to manage the *resources*: a matter of operation and a difficult task needing a variety of professional skills.

Resource management starts with the preparation of an effective and realistic policy, and then a plan with related strategies for development and marketing which must be prepared together. Experts are available to help in this work, and should be chosen carefully to ensure competence and experience.

The implementation of the plan requires expertise of a different kind. There are skilled management consultants specialising in international traffic whose work can be supported by the appropriate official international agency.

A vital part of their work must be to advise on the role, selection and partnership agreements of foreign developers including multinational companies. This will involve the offer of a package of *national benefits* by the government concerned including guaranteed repatriation of capital and profits, security of investment and tenure, fair operating conditions, the right to employ foreign management and other skilled labour, and favourable taxation. It is, for example, common to waive import duty on materials and supplies and sometimes give freedom from company or personal taxes.

Subsidies for capital investment may also be appropriate. The agreement for joint schemes to attract foreign operators needs commercial management with great experience and competence, to ensure a harmonious partnership balancing benefits for the territory and justifiable rewards or profits for the risks taken and investment made by the foreign companies. They in turn have scarce resources, and must choose one scheme for expansion rather than another. This will be determined by their company plan for their own greater prosperity.

It is not a question of right and wrong, exploitation or protecting national interests, but rather the effective selection of commercial partners in international tourism development and a satisfactory management agreement to share risk and profit. There can be many forms of co-operation, joint schemes, agency or franchise agreements to full international commercial investment. There are quantifiable pros and cons for each form of investment. The government must consider long term costs and benefits in their development plan before making agreements with commercial partners. It is also advisable, in view of the volatile nature of much tourism trade in developing countries to agree from the outset some form of appraisal and review of progress which would allow for revision of the tourism plan and the obligation and rewards of the respective partners.

In many cases multinational companies' operations in developing countries may be regarded as relatively small or marginal to their main commercial strategies. Accordingly risks disproportionate to anticipated profits may require some discounting through subsidies or favourable tax and other conditions for investment, as already indicated. There are a number of possible incentive schemes, examples of which were examined in a report for the WTO by Jonathan Bodlender.[4]

There can be essential requirements such as the employment of skilled foreign staff, and the ability to import equipment, food and drink etc. taking into account that the clientele will come largely from the richer countries of the world and expect international standards of service, if tourism potential is to be fully exploited.

The developing countries can benefit greatly from such foreign investment, and may well be unable to do without such support backed up by management skills and marketing resources. The material rewards can be great but the government must act responsibly as the guardian or owner of the national destination. It has a great responsibility to manage the national tourist resources effectively, and to invest wisely in expert advisors help.

It is essential for successful international trading to make the right agreements, and to discount risk appropriately through effective subsidies, grants, guarantees or other state facilities. But to strike the right balance, and avoid giving away too much needs professionalism and business experience. Ignorance, impatience and the lure of short term political advantage can be costly and may be disastrous. But these errors are often the cause of disappointing results in tourism programmes in third world countries rather than the fault of multinational companies.

There is criticism that the companies can be too greedy, that their activities may result in considerable *leakage* of foreign currency and profits, and that they cannot be relied upon for long term support if conditions change. These potential problems or obligations should be dealt with at the outset by choosing competent partners and agreeing terms of partnership with professional guidance. *Leakage* of foreign currency is a misleading term. All foreign investment and sophisticated trades and industry require imported resources including raw materials and skilled labour as well as capital. Such costs will be an essential part of any successful industrial development, particularly when exploiting new resources. Tourism may in fact prove more cost effective in its use of scarce foreign investment for creating additional national prosperity than alternatives in primary or manufacturing industry. Studies have shown that the *import* content is usually much lower for tourism, a labour intensive service trade, than in most manufacturing trades. It can be lower than 10 per cent of producer costs in industrialised countries (excluding international transport). Furthermore in the third world countries there may not be better alternative economic resources for growth, and few if any that offer additional benefits in indirect employment and regional prosperity. Expansion of the visitor trade can create many secondary and support businesses stimulated by the lead of a few major internationally funded projects. Foreign companies can also help train the local work force to fill new jobs in an expanding business including management.

Reference

1 *Current Travel and Tourism Indicators* WTO 1990
Yearbook of Tourism Statistics Vol I Vol II (1988 and annual) WTO
2 *Tourism Policy and International Tourism in OECD Member Countries* OECD Paris 1989
3 *Tourism Facing Change*, L J Lickorish Horwath Book of Tourism MacMillan Press 1990
4 *Guidelines on Tourism Investment* WTO 1980

Appendix

Definition of tourism

Professor Medlik of the University of Surrey put forward the following definition – 'the phenomenon arising from temporary visits (or staying away from home) outside the normal place of residence for any reason other than following an occupation remunerated from within the place visited'. This fits well with the official international definitions and is suitable for international and national studies.

In 1968 the Statistical Commission of the United Nations approved the following:

> for statistical purposes the term 'visitor' describes any person visiting a country other than that in which he has his usual place of residence for any reason other than following an occupation remunerated from within the country visited

The International Union of Official Tourist Organisations (IUOTO), later to become the World Tourist Organisation (WTO) supported this description, but recommended that the term 'visitor' should be divided into two categories, 'tourists' to include visitors making at least one overnight stay, and 'excursionists' or in other words, day visitors.

> Tourist, ie. temporary visitor staying at least twenty-four hours in the country visited, the purpose of whose journey can be classified under one of the following headings:
>
> 1. Leisure (recreation, holiday, health, study, religion and sport)
> 2. Business, family, mission, meeting.
>
> Excursionist, ie. temporary visitor staying less than twenty-four hours in the country visited (including travellers on cruises). The statistics should not include travellers, who in the legal sense do not enter the country (air travellers who do not leave an airport's transit area and similar cases).

These definitions were intended for use in measuring international travel and fitted into the police, immigration and frontier control systems. But they are basically economic and also work well for domestic travel, at least in theory. The key feature is the expenditure by the visitor at the destination, which represents an injection of revenue (income) from outside the territory ie.

region, town or resort. Thus the essential concept of tourism is economic. It can best be seen, studied and worked at as a market, as an economic entity which gives the activity its identity.

Part IV: Planning in action

Jonathan Bodlender

12 Examples of tourist planning

The development of tourism, to a country or region, involves the provision of a multitude of interdependent services. Whilst the economic benefits of tourism are widely recognised, the investment necessary to reap these benefits is substantial. The key to successful tourism development lies in careful planning. This section examines the elements of tourism planning through reference to selected assignments which Horwath Consulting has carried out in countries with both established and developing tourism industries.

Tourism planning has changed considerably in recent years. Whereas previously planning involved the preparation of extensive master plans, often taking several years to complete, these have now been replaced by strategies which more resemble a company business plan. Objectives are targeted and recommendations to achieve these given timeframes in which to be completed. Furthermore, many of the agencies funding tourism development plans (such as the Commission of the European Community and the United Nations) are insisting on proper emphasis being put on training and marketing.

The following case studies have all been drawn from the files and records of Horwath Consulting Ltd (formerly named Horwath & Horwath (UK) Ltd). They illustrate the interdependence of the various components of tourism planning including physical planning, human resources, marketing and organisation of tourism management. The countries chosen range from a developing country with an emerging tourist industry, to an important West European country with a long established and highly reputed tourism industry. The work carried out varies from master plans to a study to determine the hotel development requirements of a single city, and also studies which deal with marketing. While each country is very different, the essential components of tourism planning are common to all of them.

Case Study 1: Bali, Nusa Dua

This assignment was carried out for the Bali Tourism Development Corporation, an agency of the Indonesian government, at the instigation, and with the support, of the World Bank in 1977/78. The project was to consider the style, type and cost of hotels to be built at Nusa Dua, Bali's designated tourism development area.

Already $100 million at mid-late 1970s values had been spent on superstructure and infrastructure which was almost complete, without, surprisingly enough, this analysis having been carried out. Over the years there had been consultants dealing with the project as a whole from its inception, with Bali's transportation and various other matters. All the thinking and previous reports, were based on the assumption of the continuance of the existing visitor patterns (made up largely of expatriates based in Djakarta and other large centres) – particularly an average length of stay of about two and a half days – with the belief that the main potential market lay in Australia and Japan. Widespread market research resulted in the following conclusions:

> The existing visitor pattern and particularly the average length of stay which presently existed was irrelevant. Supply was about to increase several fold and yet the thinking was based on the existing relatively small demand patterns.

The largest potential market at that time lay in Western Europe. The potential United States market was significant, but probably smaller. The potential Japanese market was for group overnight stops and, perhaps reflecting the absence of what might be termed a sex industry, was fairly modest. And the potential Australian market was really very modest indeed, reflecting a lack of interest in the culture, and Australia's own excellent beaches; most Australian interviewees in Bali also cited the cost of beer!

Having regard to the derivation the market, many of the visitors would come by long-haul traffic both as a single destination and part of a multi-destination visit. If the latter, as part of the multi-destination visit, Bali would probably provide the turn-round point and therefore benefit from a visit both for combined cultural purposes and also the two or three beach based days which are usually included in these tours.

It was calculated that the average length of stay in Bali would become some six days – not two and a half as previously thought.

As a corollary to this it was necessary for the hotels to incorporate leisure facilities such as tennis courts and good swimming pools. An additional pattern of thought had been that as guests did not use too frequently the beaches and the swimming pools in the existing hotels, it was unlikely that they would do so in future; that these were generally very poor indeed and exceptionally uninviting had not occurred to anybody.

As an additional corollary there were very distinct implications for the airport and the airport terminal. Because if, say, 65 per cent room occupancy was going to be achieved with X thousand rooms in Bali at an average stay of six days, there would be many less arrivals than if the same occupancy was achieved with an average length of stay of two and a half days. This had not seemed to occur to the Indonesian government, which was basing its airport planning on a previous transport study which seemed to adopt passenger arrival and departure numbers derived from an assumed hotel occupancy and length of stay for the intended new hotel capacity, without an actual market study to confirm or deny the assumptions.

The only basic change in policy which would enable private sector investment in hotels to be profitable was also agreed as a result of the study but in this case related to cash flow analysis rather than market influences. It was necessary for the Indonesian government to agree to waive import duty on capital equipment which in turn resulted in a reduction of total capital costs of 30 per cent to make investment a viable proposition. This particular factor in the study was eventually accepted.

The study for Bali was completed in 1978. New hotel construction was somewhat delayed, although it has since taken place. But it was possible to judge that the market assessment was correct because over the next few years, demand first from Western Europe and later from the United States for Thailand, which offered a comparable product (a combination of cultural and beach based tourism) increased substantially. It was only much later that demand from Japan and Australia was to grow in line with distinct changes in the travel patterns of these countries.

Case Study 2: Thailand

Shortly afterwards, in 1981/82, an assignment was carried out for the Tourism Authority of Thailand which had recognised the need for a thorough assessment of its overseas marketing in its main, and potentially main demand generating areas. Who was actually *selling* the visit: airline, wholesaler, retailer? Was it different in different countries? How effective was the selling? Could the selling arrangements, or the official support for them, be improved? Had the cultural aspects of selling been observed?

With this brief the following was then examined:

- The perception of the tourist product in various European countries which made up the main potential demand generating areas;
- Difficulties which arose from any image problem and misunderstanding of the product because of this: in effect the capital city had an image as a sex tour destination which was having an adverse affect on the family market in some European countries.

We discovered that although the capital and its surrounding area offers an adequate and indeed outstanding product which includes the charms of a city with cultural and historical attractions together with excellent shopping, art and communications combined with nearby resort areas both coastal, island and mountain. Nevertheless it was inadequately packaged and presented to the market.

The national tourist authorities completely misunderstood western marketing, and that which is inherent in it – including the costs generally and particularly the cost of advertising. As an example, the total annual allocation for advertising in Germany would have purchased only one minute of advertising on German television at peak time.

Because of a shortage of promotional material, tourist leaflets promoting Thailand in France were written and circulated in English.

Thailand offers a similar product to Bali and soon after our study experienced a similar geographical pattern of demand to that which we had forecast earlier for Bali.

But the sex industry had begun to become a problem for Thailand by creating a poor image of the country abroad, and so deterring family holidays from some potentially important generating countries.

Case Study 3: Stockholm, Sweden

The possibility of Stockholm becoming an international convention centre was under discussion. So a report was prepared in 1978 for the city of Stockholm updated in 1981 on its hotel development requirements based on 3 scenarios:

- A new 2,500 seat conference centre;
- A new 1,500 seat conference centre;
- No new conference centre

It was calculated that a new first class hotel would need to achieve a 50 per cent increase in average room rates over the norm being experienced to result in a pay back period of eight years, an acceptable, albeit unexciting, internal rate of return. And this was so, although the present unsatisfied demand together with potential increases over the next decade would support a substantial number of new rooms, and that without a new conference centre. Indeed, a new conference centre would create demand only in months when maximum occupancy would be achieved anyway.

However, the position in Stockholm was not as black as it seemed. Against a background of high labour costs (payroll was running at 45 per cent of turnover), an 85 per cent average annual room occupancy, and during mid-week a largely price insensitive, business oriented demand, the report emphasised that prevailing room rack rates were much too low. A hotel must become more profitable, if, say, a 50 per cent increase in room rates results only in a drop in occupancy from 85 per cent to say 60 per cent. One leading hotel then substantially raised its room prices with no fall off in business – in fact an increase in occupancy was achieved!

Case Study 4: Sweden's Holiday Product

Later, in 1984, on behalf of the Swedish Hotel and Restaurant Association, research was carried out to ascertain how the Swedish hotel and restaurant product was perceived by foreign visitors to Sweden. The purpose of the analysis was to produce recommendations which, if acted upon, would enable the Swedish hotels and restaurants to increase demand for the Swedish holiday product and for the share of the accommodation market in Sweden. The research conducted was of a qualitative nature and was based upon:

1. Responses of Swedish hoteliers and foreign tour operators to a standard questionnaire; and
2. Results of detailed personal interviews conducted throughout Western Europe with members of the travel trade.

The results of the research showed that fundamentally the product, ie Swedish hotels and restaurants, was up to the standard expected by foreign visitors but that the marketing of Swedish hotels to the foreign travel trade was inadequate, particularly when compared with the marketing of overseas competitors, and also of Swedish self-catering accommodation.

The main recommendations were:

- Hotels should be promoted in isolation, but that hoteliers should join forces with tour operators, ferry companies, airlines and the tourist boards to promote Sweden, and even Scandinavia. Greater co-operation was needed between all sectors involved to present a united front to the purchaser of the Swedish tourism product.

- The marketing of hotels was fragmented and the resources needed to be pooled if it was to be more effective.
- A hotel classification system should be implemented to improve communication of standards and style between hotels, the travel trade and the end user.
- As far as the product was concerned, the restrictions on the service of alcohol, more perhaps than the high tax, were perceived to be a major problem.
- It was recommended that steps should be taken to counteract the expensive prevailing image of Sweden, and that hoteliers and restaurateurs needed to beware of over-pricing themselves in the holiday market.

It will be noted that the recommendations were mainly towards more effective marketing.

Case Study 5: Troodos and Hill Resorts, Cyprus

In recent years there had been a rapid growth of international tourism to Cyprus, growth which had occurred almost entirely at the coast, while the Troodos mountain region, and the central hill resorts in particular, had not participated in this trend.

The Cyprus government wished to diversify away from the predominantly beach based tourism which was being experienced. But at the same time it was concerned at fragmented and environmentally damaging development in the Troodos region.

A report, commissioned by the Commonwealth Secretariat in 1989 was prepared for the Cyprus Tourism Organisation assessing short and medium term objectives for the Troodos and hill resort areas. The study comprised a detailed review of all appropriate development factors and their interaction on the ecological, social and economic structure of the region. The study also addressed a number of the following sub-objectives:

- Improvement of profitability and seasonality of existing accommodation units;
- Improvements to the quality of the tourist product;
- Marketing and promotion of the study area with a view to decongesting the coastal regions;
- Identification of investment opportunities.

During the course of our extensive research it was apparent that despite the existence of a variety of tourism access and activities, the environment of the mountain region had been adversely affected in recent years by two major factors. First, the emigration of the rural population to coastal towns and the capital, Nicosia and, secondly, the improvement of access from the same towns into the mountain villages. The first factor had resulted in a decline in the standard of maintenance of the villages and the countryside, while the second factor had led to the development of second homes for urban dwellers, and increase of facilities to cater for day trippers had resulted in environmental damage and a complete change in the character of the area.

Previous development proposals were highly ambitious and virtually none of them had been implemented, although they involved the investment of considerable sums of money. There was therefore a lack of both investment in tourism facilities and any defined physical or strategic framework against which projects could be assessed and, where appropriate, implemented.

The overall recommended strategy was to:

- Maintain and, where possible, restore the region's natural environment and traditional village character;
- Develop places of interest as attractions for international tourists;
- Develop facilities for domestic recreational visitors and day excursionists.

Creation of a readily definable image for the region was regarded as an important strategic consideration in order to increase competitiveness in the international tourism market place.

The recommended strategy was in our opinion consistent with market requirements and would also represent a means of encouraging conservation rather than conflicting with it. The strategy also was directed at the main geographical components of the Troodos and Hills regions. In summary, our strategy was to create a low-key, dispersed pattern of development and to encourage a process of organic growth in tourism and recreation in a harmonious fashion, without conflicts arising either between different interest groups or the environment. The strategy was therefore evolutionary rater than revolutionary.

Main projects recommended as being necessary for realisation of the overall strategy included:

- Creation of a Troodos National Park;
- Encouragement of a new ski centre;
- Improvements to tourist information;

- Provision of an interpretation centre;
- General environmental improvements;
- Implementations of a marketing promotion programme.

Threefold strengths arising from the implementation of our proposals would be:

- Economic
- Social
- Environmental

Principal benefits were likely to be environmental and, provided that tourism and recreation were allowed to develop in a controlled, orderly and dispersed fashion as recommended, the report anticipated that the suggested programme of activities would provide a major impetus to the preservation of the environment for future generations to enjoy.

The Cyprus government has implemented parts of the report, and still has other parts under consideration.

Case Study 6: Malta

Malta already had a long established hotel industry, but the government, with the support of the operational sector, decided that it was appropriate for the tourism industry to be comprehensively reassessed and that a tourism master plan should be prepared outlining new strategies, policies and initiatives to be adopted. Financial support for this was forthcoming from the World Tourism Organisation with the actual funding being provided by UNDP, and the report was completed in 1989.

The plan involved both product and market reassessment from which the strategies, policies and development objectives could be derived. It was agreed at the outset that the master plan had to be market orientated. The product had to be market lead.

A major constraint on the size, and influence on the type, of future tourism to Malta was provided by both the relatively small size of the Maltese Islands and also a population of only 350,000. This population was already receiving 780,000 visitors annually (1988).

It was soon agreed that Malta would not wish to receive many more tourists by number, and that any increases should be in the shoulder months and low season rather than in the congested high season.

Similarly, every effort needed to be made to improve the quality of tourism, in order that average spends should be higher, and that this was more important than increasing numbers, particularly in the busy summer months.

It was readily apparent that there was too much reliance on the large British market. Malta was therefore vulnerable to swings in the British market, swings which could be outside Maltese control such as a recession in the UK.
Amongst the strategies that were recommended were therefore to:

- Improve the quality of the product, and at the same time lengthen the season. This was to be achieved by a number of methods including the encouragement of specialised watersports and activities. For example Malta already had an excellent reputation for scuba diving and this in itself offered potential in what tends to be a high spending market. Yachting also was seen as providing potential.
- Sports, cultural and other attractions were seen as providing opportunities, including cultural tourism, perhaps as part of winter multi-destination visits for example linking with other Mediterranean Island such as the nearby Sicily, Crete, and Cyprus.
- Encouragement of conference business was foreseen.
- A number of potential new developments were discussed with the aid of an international and a local planner in the team advising on the environmental aspects. Conservation of a number of sites was another issue addressed in the report.

The report recognised the importance of human resources to the tourism industry and in particular the need to improve the image and career structure of the industry. It recommended:

- Active industrial involvement in training;
- Proposals for operational aspects of the Institute of Tourism Studies;
- More overseas placements for management trainees;
- Launch of a tourism awareness programme for schools;
- Creation of more attractive career structures in the tourism industry;
- increased funding by the private sector of the training institution.

It is obviously early days yet to review the effects of a plan the objectives and strategies of which will be developed over the period 1990–2005. However, tourism results for 1990 indicate that visitor arrivals will increase by some 5 per cent over 1989 and that already some success has been achieved in reducing over-reliance upon the UK market – down by some 7 per cent. In contrast, and in line with the recommendations, the German share of the market has increased considerably.

Other parts of the tourism strategy that have already been implemented include the moving of the various tourism departments together under one roof in Valetta.

Case Study 7: Switzerland

A report on the future of Switzerland's foreign tourism was prepared in 1989/90. As an integral part of the report, the socioeconomic and demographic patterns of Switzerland's main markets and potential main markets were to be examined. For example, demographic changes in what was then West Germany in particular were expected to benefit Switzerland which was drawing nearly 50 per cent of its foreign tourism arrivals from there – mainly from older people.

Switzerland has had a long and established tourism industry. It currently ranked in eighth place internationally in terms of tourism receipts though its share of tourism arrivals declined between 1982 and 1988.

The research revealed that a level of complacency was evident in the Swiss tourism industry. It had been so successful, for so long that hoteliers, and other involved in tourism, had begun to rest on their laurels and failed to recognise new competitor countries and regions which were emerging with modern products, well packaged and presented.

The interviewing of foreign wholesalers indicated a danger of product obsolescence; it also revealed an efficient, but sterile, image.

Interviewing within Switzerland revealed a lack of concern with marketing, particularly amongst hoteliers where a lack of marketing awareness was perceived. The report identified a number of areas for improvement, in particular:

- Offering *state of the art* (ie not obsolete or outmoded) products;
- Lengthening the season, particularly in the highly seasonal resorts. Conference business was cited as offering potential towards achieving this;
- Marketing effectively, particularly:
  1. Enhanced awareness, and perhaps even a change of 'culture', amongst hoteliers;
  2. Improved co-ordination generally;
  3. Use of the latest technology and techniques.
- Improving the image of the industry – particularly in the context of human resources.

Switzerland also suffered from lack of co-ordination in its marketing between national, Cantonal and city officials, and tourist offices, and also between these and the various parts of the operational sector – airline, hoteliers, ground handlers, etc.

The report indicated that it was necessary to improve marketing awareness and techniques substantially at all levels of the tourist industry. These techniques internationally were becoming much more sophisticated, and *state of the art* electronics in the form of the *mega* computer reservation systems such as Amadeus, Galilleo and Sabre were anticipated to have a major impact on international marketing.

Switzerland displayed a pronounced pattern of tourist seasonality due to the different products it offers in winter and summer. This seasonality impacted on the various tourist regions since certain regions catered only for winter or summer tourism. The report recommended that the infrastructure currently in place for winter tourism and representing substantial investment be used to attract conference and incentive tourism in the low and shoulder season months. The use of snow machines to guarantee skiing throughout the winter was also recommended.

The report was published in November 1990. It remains to be seen how Swiss tourism will develop in the future.

13 Project appraisal and financing

This chapter is concerned with the relationships between project appraisal and financing. The objectives of which are to examine the role of consultants and professional advisors and highlight the criteria used by commercial financing institutions in assessing the viability of projects for funding.

Within the context above, we discuss the effects of government tourism investment incentives and grant aid, matters which are of special relevance to developing countries, whilst examining the principal methods by which governments can produce financial aid for tourism projects. This, essentially is concerned with the relationships between governments and private sector investment. The chapter concentrates on new project financing generally, and on hotel project presentation and assessment. It draws widely on *An Examination of Tourism Investment Incentives* by Jonathan Bodlender and Trevor Ward, published in February 1987 by World Tourism Organisation and Horwath & Horwath International.

Why commission a feasibility study?

As the number of hotel projects submitted for consideration to financing institutions increases each year, so does the need to present projects with the relevant and necessary information for these institutions to make their decisions.

Most financing institutions require an independent market and financial feasibility study for a proposed development. Although they will usually conduct some research of their own, and indeed are quite capable of preparing a feasibility study for themselves, using internal resources, it is unusual for them to carry out the depth of research required for a full market and financial feasibility study. Aside from the fact, that to do this is not an effective use of their time and skills, it is difficult for them to be independent of a project when they stand to gain by a project going ahead, for example, a successful deal may help to meet or exceed budget and thereby possibly act as an incentive to increase individual bonuses.

It is under these circumstances that professional advisors, or in the context of hotels, experienced hotel consultants are called upon to prepare a feasibility study for a proposed new development. A professional consultant can offer, to the process of preparing a feasibility study three qualities, one or more of which is missing from all other parties to the development. These are independence, objectivity, and experience: measured in terms of personal experience as well as support services such as a comprehensive data bank.

Let us go back now and look at what exactly is a feasibility study?

What is a feasibility study?

The purpose of a feasibility study is to provide:

1. an objective analysis of the project under consideration, including the environment for the project;
2. a document prepared to examine the market conditions in which the project will operate;
3. an appraisal of the investment opportunity.[1]

The need for an independent feasibility study will depend on whether the study is:

Mechanical – these are studies which a client commissions because third parties require it of him. The client would not otherwise have commissioned a study, and therefore has no personal use *per se* for the information or recommendations therein. The source of finance may require a prospective borrower to provide an independent feasibility study in support of the application for funds, and this is the most common circumstance in which a *mechanical* study is prepared. Bankers, certainly are reluctant to accept project appraisals prepared by advisors such as architects or quantity surveyors, and are less willing to lend on projects unless they have been well researched and have been carried out by independent professional organisations.

Pro-active – where the client who commissions the study requires information to be provided in addition to projections of the return on investment. For example, the study may be required to define the concept of the hotel, or to provide marketing and operational information.

In general, however, it is possible to categorise the reasons that feasibility studies are commissioned into seven groups. Few hotel feasibility studies fall into one group only, some cover the entire range.

1. To demonstrate that a project is viable.
2. To support an application for finance.
3. To support an application for planning permission.
4. To attract potential operators.
5. To define optimum land use.
6. To define a concept.
7. To present to other parties (eg a board of directors or as the basis of a circular or prospectus).

Key elements of feasibility study

A feasibility study will usually consist of the following key elements:

1. ***General background information*** – this covers key data including background to the country, region and location for the proposed hotel, together with economic and demographic information. It will also include an examination of existing, and likely future tourism trends to the area. This information comes from research and published data. Sources include government departments, municipalities, chambers of commerce, airport authorities and other similar organisations.
2. ***Site evaluation*** – this is based on a physical inspection of the site and its surroundings, taking into consideration its location, accessibility to utilities and infrastructure such as transportation. The physical characteristics of the site including its topology and topography are also considered.

   In certain circumstances, input from other professionals such as civil engineers might be required. Environmental factors including the site's general suitability in terms of its size, land shape and configuration are studied. Consideration has also to be given to the type of site: green field, built-up area, town centre, motorway junction, beach, resort, mountain, airport and sports facilities eg golf.
3. ***Market assessment – accommodation*** – looks at current and historic market demand, and its major characteristics which can be analysed in market segments: business, conference, holiday, sports, air crews, etc. Within each segment, the guest profile, nationality, seasonality, length of stay and double occupancy factors are surveyed.

   In looking at market demand a differentiation is made between demand which occurs in that location, such as businessmen visiting local companies, people attending a particular sporting event or air crew demand generated by the local airport or, demand which is created or attracted into the area, such as conferences and holidaymakers who may have a choice of venues or destinations.

Market evaluation determines the existing supply and assesses the relevant competitive supply based on the product, reputation, appraisal, positioning and the markets they attract. The analysis of the trading performance of competitive hotels look closely at the pricing structure which includes published tariffs, annual increases, discounting policies and price sensitivity, both during weekend and midweek, which effect the achieved average room rate.

The quantification of existing demand, looks at the current market situation and whether demand is satisfied, or displaced and hence dissatisfied.

The assessment of quantification and profile of demand is based on interviews with hoteliers in the relevant market areas, from research with demand generators such as local companies, tour operators, representatives of transport companies, conference organisers, and also from other parties including tourist boards or the tourism ministry.

The assessment of future supply or planned additions is based on interviews with tourist officials, hoteliers, hotel companies, planning officials and others. It looks at those relevant projects and their proposed facilities in relationship to the existing market and whether there is a *threat* to the proposed project under construction.

Included in the market evaluation is an assessment of future demand which looks at the likely market share and demand potential taking account of potential new markets eg conferences, and new trends eg weekend breaks. Future demand evaluation will also draw on the assessment of the local national economy, the climate for tourism development, transportation and traffic, and other factors.

Finally, within the market assessment will be a survey of all other facilities including food and beverage, banqueting, functions, special events, the provision of sports facilities and their utilisation and types of memberships; entertainment facilities and rentals; and other income including shops, offices, and commission.

4. ***Project information*** – this may be based on a scheme put forward by the promoter, with comments and recommendations from the consultants or it may be recommendations starting afresh. The information will cover the design concept and recommended facilities, eg rooms, restaurants, bars, conference/function rooms, business centre etc, and comment on the proposed hotel's position in the market. This

section may also make recommendations as to the type of management and marketing that is most appropriate to the hotel.

5. ***Projected profit and loss statements*** – which includes all other revenues and expenses to gross operating profit.

   The operating statistics for the proposed development come from specific research in the market area, other relevant data and experiences and, in some cases, input from the proposed operator. It covers:

   Cost of sales
   - Food;
   - Beverage;
   - Telephone and telex;
   - Other facilities.

   Expenses by department
   - Staffing and payroll costs;
   - Management fee.

   Market penetration assessment
   The assessment of market penetration, covering both specific local markets and demand attracted into the area, comes from the market research and product recommendations, and relies on the judgement of the team preparing the study.
   In some cases, this would involve marketing input from the operator of the hotel.

   - Fair share analysis;
   - Occupancy/market build-up;
   - Created demand;
   - Pricing;
   - Facilities;
   - Management and marketing;
   - Calculation of room nights sold and average room occupancy;
   - Calculation of average room rate;
   - Cost of sales;
   - Distributed expenses;
   - Undistributed expenses;
   - Payroll or related expenses

6. ***Financial viability assessment*** – cash flow projections for the project are based on preliminary estimates of capital costs and an assumed method of financing.

   Capital cost information would be provided by a Quantity Surveyor if the scheme is well advanced, or could, for an initial cash flow projection, be based on rule of thumb estimates for the type of hotel and location.

Likewise the finance plan can be based on a financing proposal or alternatively a reasonable, albeit hypothetic finance plan. The investment/finance criteria is discussed in more detail later in this chapter.

Major factors affecting viability

Clearly all steps in the preparation of a feasibility are important. However, major factors affecting the viability of a project include:

1. The appropriateness of the site;
2. Optimising the average annual room occupancy and achieved average room rate;
3. Operational efficiency – particularly staffing and payroll;
4. Gearing the finance plan to the projected income stream.

Timing of the hotel feasibility study[1]

Often the preparation of a hotel feasibility study is viewed as a defined step on the development ladder which, once used, is no longer required. This may be because the client already has the resources to attract an operator, to define the concept and identify market opportunities, but needs a feasibility study to support an application for finance. In this case the developer may well not derive maximum benefit from the study. To be of greatest value, a hotel feasibility study should be a continuing tool in the development process. The exact sequence of events will vary with circumstances, but the following phased project development process is an indication of the way events could run:

1. Preliminary concept (including an idea of capital costs);
2. Assemble Players including:
   - operator
   - finance
   - construction
3. Market study;
4. Revised concept;
5. Revised costings;
6. Financial Evaluation of Project;
7. Sensitivity analyses;
8. Financing arrangements;
9. Detailed design and planning;
10. Project Implementation.

In this model, 3, 4 and 6 are consecutive phases of the feasibility study. There would be a loop to the model, allowing for a revision of the concept if the financial evaluation produced unacceptable results.

Conclusion of a feasibility study

A feasibility study may well be presented to more than one source, the measure of feasibility used could therefore differ which makes it difficult for a consultant to reach any conclusion.

The most common reason for commissioning a study is to support an application for finance, indeed, nearly all studies are used for this purpose. In this context, a feasibility study evaluates a project on the basis of income and shows the capability of the project to meet debt service and equity requirements. However,

> The financial projections, based upon the development proposal (which must be closely defined by the report), will represent the view of the author of that study as to what can reasonably be expected, and the methods used to calculate those projections, and the conditions upon which they depend, must also be carefully detailed. These financial projections do not represent forecasts, in that they will not have the degree of certainty required by forecasts (they are also generally too far in the future to be accurate in that respect); nor do the financial projections represent budgets for management to work with once the hotel is open, for the same reason. They do represent an evaluation, under present and projected future conditions as defined by the report, of how the consultant, who should have depth and breadth of knowledge of the subject, views the development in financial terms.
>
> However, the future can never be predicted with guaranteed accuracy and although the consultant will bring his experience into the equation when doing so, and will conscientiously research all the factors which might impact on future projections, unforeseen events can and will happen. Such things might be the unexpected closure of a major employer and generator of rooms demand, perhaps because the firm has been taken over and operations moved elsewhere; or a natural disaster, such as an earthquake, which destroys half the existing hotel stock in a moment.
>
> The findings of a hotel feasibility study should therefore be subject to examination at regular intervals to assess the impact of any changes in the bases and conditions of the recommendations and projections which have been built up on those factors.[2]

Investment criteria for a specific project

The main investment criteria for a specific project is the ability of that project to generate sufficient profit, financial returns and cash flow to service the investment, both in terms of return on equity and loan interest and repayments.

Financing structure

In general, the means of financing hotel projects on a commercial basis is through a mixture of loan finance and equity finance.

Loan Finance – is finance, bearing interest (which may be either fixed at the commencement of the loan or which varies according to the market rate of interest) and requiring predetermined repayment and security. It is increasingly common for the completed hotel to become the security for the loan. This is known as non-recourse borrowing since the lender has no recourse to any other assets of the borrower in the event of the project's failure.

Equity Finance – the risk sharing part of the company's capital. The level of equity involvement by a particular investor determines their share of the ownership of the company. Equity investors receive a part of the reserved profits in proportion to their share in the equity of the company. Unlike a loan, there is no guaranteed repayment and the equity investor is speculating on the success of the company. Equity investment is also known as risk capital.

Most loan finance is raised through banks, either Clearing Banks or Merchant Banks specialising in lending money for new projects. Many of these Merchant Banks have divisions which specialise in assessing hotel and leisure projects. A commercial lending institution's prime interest will be the project's ability to service its (and other) loans throughout the terms of these loans.

Equity Finance for a new project can either come from existing cash flow (if it is a company wishing to expand), or it can be raised through equity brokers. In a number of countries fiscal incentives exist to encourage equity participation in hotel and tourism projects. Equity investors will mainly be interested in the level of the return they will receive on their capital, and will probably expect an element of *risk return*.

Cash Flow

The statement of estimated cash flow for a project records the deductions from gross operating profit prior to taxation and return on equity investment. They are usually inflated to give actual year values.

A typical cash flow statement would include the following deductions from Gross Operating Profit:

• Ground rent	:	The rent payable on the site of the hotel
• Building insurance	:	Usually assumed as a percentage of the construction cost of the hotel.
• Replacement of furniture fittings and equipment (FF&E).	:	Calculated as a percentage of the initial cost of of the FF&E
• Management incentive fee	:	If the hotel is operated by a management company it is usual for a fee related to gross operating profit to be paid to the management company.
• Repayments	:	Loan repayments can either be in equal instalments over the term of the loan or involve more or less of the loan repaid at the earlier or later stages of its life.
• Interest	:	It is usual to assume a fixed rate of interest in assessing the level of interest to be paid each year

These deductions from Gross Operating Profit give the annual surplus (before taxation). It is usual also to show the cumulative surplus (before taxation). This shows the length of time needed to recoup the equity investment in the project.

It should be noted that if the financing for the project is in a *Hard* currency the cash flow should show the levels of Hard Currency which the project will produce to service the debt and return on equity required by foreign investors.

Appraising the cash flow

To secure the loan finance it is essential to demonstrate that the cash flow will be sufficient to comply with the terms of the loan. For any equity investment in a hotel there are three main means of measuring its attractiveness as follows:

1. ***Return on capital employed*** – also known as the Accounting Rate of Return. It is calculated as the ratio of the average annual profit from an investment project expressed as a percentage of the original capital invested. This investment appraisal technique is widely used in practice. It has three main advantages:

(a) Management are familiar with evaluating a project on the basis of a percentage rate of return.
(b) It evaluates the project on its profitability which management often believe should be the focus of the appraisal.
(c) Shareholders often evaluate management's performance on the company's overall return on capital. Therefore it is fairly logical to evaluate individual capital investment opportunities on a similar basis.

2. ***Payback period*** – this is one of the most well used and trusted methods of investment appraisal. It refers to the number of years to recoup the initial capital invested. This method does not take account of an effective devaluation of the original capital due to inflation. The higher the risk of the project, the shorter the payback period required. Main advantages of the payback method are:
   (a) Quick and simple to calculate (once the project's cash flow forecasts have been made) and is easily understood by management.
   (b) Projects can be ranked in terms of 'speed of payback' the more quickly a project achieves payback, the less risky the project. Management can therefore quickly select the less risky project.
   (c) Payback avoids having to forecast cash flows over the whole of the project's life which is difficult and is more so the further ahead in time the forecast has to be made.
   (d) It is a convenient method to use in 'capital rationing' situations when a company does not have unlimited capital expenditure funds. If capital is short, then arguably the most sensible projects to accept are those which return the expenditure rapidly.
3. ***Discounted Cash Flow*** – discounting the cash flow places greater relative value on surpluses earned in earlier years.

   Present Values – the present value of money earned in the future takes account of the fact that money earned in the future has a cost attached to it in the form of interest. Calculating the present value of future income involves *removing* the interest component from a future income stream. By adding the present value of each year's surplus (inflows) to the capital expenditure (outflow) the net present value (NPV) may be calculated. If the NPV is greater than zero this indicates a cash surplus after interest and an acceptable project. Different projects may be assessed by examining their Net Present Values: the higher the NPV, the more attractive the project.

Internal Rate of Return – the internal rate of return is the rate of return which gives a net present value of zero. It is the return on investment which makes the total inflows and the residual value equal to the initial capital outflow. The value of this is that it gives the true rate of return on a project. If this rate is less than the rate of interest available then the project would not be viable.

It should be noted that a change in the proportion of equity and loan finance for a project (the gearing) can significantly alter the results of the above analyses.

In addition, lengthening of the term of the loan so reducing the annual repayments can have the same, or an improved effect on the viability of a project than an equivalent reduction in interest rate.

Generally, cash flow surpluses are small during the initial operating periods when debt service tends to be greatest. It is often necessary to arrange the terms of repayment to allow a moratorium during initial operating periods.

What commercial financial institutions require from hotel projects

Since banks which lend money and other financial institutions which invest money are both concerned with the possibilities for the success of a project both have similar prerequisites before deciding to invest. In addition to a feasibility study and projected cash flow the following elements of a project are also considered in appraising projects:

1. ***The 'Track record' of the developer*** – Institutions are reluctant to loan or invest in projects where they feel the developer does not have the substance to co-ordinate a particular project. Generally the higher the risk of the project the more necessary it will be to show a history of having developed projects of similar size and scale.
2. ***Appropriate management*** – Prior to funding a project, a bank or other institution will need to be satisfied that there is sufficient competent management in place to co-ordinate the development and progress of the project to opening and appropriate management thereafter to manage the hotel. In many cases they may require a named management company before agreeing to finance the project.
3. ***Fixed price contracts*** – Because they involve less risk to the lender or investor, a fixed price contract is preferable to one where only estimates of cost are provided.

4. ***Financial strength*** – Banks are primarily concerned with the ability of a particular project to service debt. However, banks are particularly concerned with *overgearing*, too high a proportion of debt to equity. They also tend to view hotels as higher risk projects than others. Because they see no alternative use for a hotel in the event of failure, it is usual to insist upon higher yields than for other industries.
5. ***Security and Collateral*** – In many cases the only security which the bank will have on a project is the completed building itself. For this reason banks will obtain an independent valuation of the hotel prior to financing the project. The valuation is usually prepared on an income basis.

Financial and Sensitivity Analysis

Financial institutions when presented with a project will conduct their own analysis, particularly of the financial aspects of the project as discussed earlier in this chapter and of the assumptions underlying the feasibility study. Projections are usually examined under three scenarios.

1. The feasibility study projections.
2. The bank's own projections – these tend to be scaled down and less optimistic.
3. A sensitivity analysis on the various projections. It involves changing one variable and examining the impact on other variables such as Gross Operating Profit and Cash Flow.

Examples

The examples which follow indicate the results of a sensitivity analysis on the cash flow for a particular project. The following assumptions have been made:

Number of rooms	150
Capital cost	$10 million
Gearing	60 per cent loan
	40 per cent equity
Interest	10 per cent
Term	10 years (equal annual installments)
Inflation	6 per cent

Rooms Revenue has been assumed as representing 45 per cent of Total Revenue. Deductions from Gross Operating Profit prior to debt service are assumed at 20 per cent of Gross Operating Profit. Values shown have been inflated to actual year values.

The summary statement of profit and loss on which the sensitivity analysis is based is as follows:

	Year 1	Year 2	Year 3
Average room occupancy (%)	55	65	70
Average rate ($)	90.00	95.40	101.12
Room revenue ($000's)	2,710	3,395	3,875
Total revenue ($000's)	6,023	7,545	8,612
Gross operating profit (%)	19	25	28

The following cumulative surpluses/deficits are achieved (in $000's), at actual year values:

Year 1	Year 2	Year 3	Year 5	Year 10
(285)	84	933	3,166	12,218

Scenario One
If a 10 per cent decrease in Average Room Occupancy is applied to this example the following changes occur:

($000's)	Year 1	Year 2	Year 3	Year 5	Year 10
Gross Operating Profit	936	1,596	2,067	2,322	3,108
Cumulative Surplus/Deficit	(451)	(314)	259	1,890	9,092

Scenario Two
With a 5 per cent decrease in Average Room Rate the following changes occur:

($000's)	Year 1	Year 2	Year 3	Year 5	Year 10
Gross Operating Profit	1,087	1,792	2,291	2,574	3,445
Cumulative Surplus/Deficit	(330)	(37)	716	2,738	11,143

Scenario Three

If both a 5 per cent decrease in Average Room Rate and 10 per cent decrease in Average Room Occupancy occur at the same time the following cash flow derives:

($000's)	Year 1	Year 2	Year 3	Year 5	Year 10
Gross Operating Profit	889	1,516	1,964	2,206	2,953
Cumulative Surplus/Deficit	(488)	(466)	75	1,526	8,173

Clearly it is possible to alter a number of variables and view their impact on the profitability and cash flow. However, it should be remembered that a sensitivity analysis acts only as a *check* on a market analysis already prepared.

Sophisticated mechanisms of funding

New and sophisticated mechanisms for funding generally involve an extension of the principles attached to loan and equity finance. Examples of such mechanisms are:

1. ***Fund investment*** – institutional investors such as Insurance Companies and Pension Funds create a special fund for the development of a particular chain or brand of hotel.
2. ***Moratorium or 'Holidays'*** – this grants a period of transition between receiving loan finance and repayment. Moratoria may be granted on either the principal repayment or on the principal and interest, usually for a period of 2 or 3 years.
3. ***'Balloon' loans*** – this form of arrangement eases the cash flow because of lower payments during the earlier term of the loan. A *balloon* is the amount left for repayment in a lump sum at the end of the loan instead of having been repaid at regular intervals during the term of the loan.
4. ***Annuity*** – an annuity spreads the principal and interest repayments equally over the term of the loan. The advantage of this is that it reduces the overall level of repayment in the early years of a project when cash flows tend to be smaller.
5. ***Sale and Leaseback*** – sale and leaseback agreements are strictly speaking a means of refinancing a project, but they are becoming increasingly important. This method involves the developer selling on the property at a profit to a third party. The money from the sale is used to repay the loan and the property is then leased from the new owner. A rental is paid each year

out of the hotels income. For a developer the advantage of this is that is realises the hotel's capital value early while at the same time providing an annual income from the hotel. In some countries there are tax advantages also to this means of financing.

Government Incentives[3]

Introduction

The investment criteria outlined in the previous section are applicable to an investment decision. If incentives offered by governments to stimulate external or private investment in their country, or a particular region of that country, are to be effective they should be aimed at meeting one or more of these criteria.

The following paragraphs relate examples of government incentives offered to help meet these investment criteria. The list is illustrative and not intended to be comprehensive.

Reducing level of required investment (investment support)

Common incentives employed by governments to stimulate tourism investment are those aimed at reducing the level of investment to be raised for a particular project. Examples are:

- Provision of land or construction labour by the government at less than market value, often in return for equity participation.
- Grants, usually with specific conditions, for a proportion of the cost of the project including, in some cases, pre-development consultation fees.
- Duty concessions on the importation of building materials, plant, furniture, fixtures and fittings.
- Investment support by the provision of funds for specific projects on favourable terms, such as over a long period of time, with low interest rates, or a combination of both. This reduces the level of investment to be raised from other sources.

Government financial incentives

Grant aid – Grant aid is considered to be the best method of *seeding* tourism projects, as it has an immediate effect upon the realisation of the project. Many tourism projects, particularly hotels and leisure centres, require a large *up-front* investment in fixed assets before operation can commence, and servicing this investment can have a serious effect upon cash flow in the early years of the project.

A grant to a tourism project may be a cash payment which does not require a return, injection of equity stake requiring profit share, or payment in kind eg, rent-free land, which would otherwise have had to have been purchased, and therefore would have required capital outlay.

Loan aid – The effect of a government loan upon a tourism project is entirely conditional upon the terms of that loan, but has a similar objective as grant aid of reducing the requirement for a developer to raise finance from other sources.

Government loan finance is most commonly given to tourism projects at preferential rates. This can be in a number of forms – interest relief schemes giving a lower interest rate, longer term, longer payment moratorium, reduced payment – *balloon* funding – all of which would be more favourable to the project than the terms available from private sector sources.

Administration of financial aid

Grant aid is the most easily administered form of financial aid for tourist projects. The awarding authority need only set the conditions for the grant, and ensure that the grant is used, and continues to be used, for the designated purpose.

Conversely loan finance requires continued administration throughout the term of the loan.

Initially, a feasibility study is required to evaluate the ability of the project to repay the loan, and this ability must be continuously re-evaluated. A mechanism is required for receiving interest and capital repayments and, because public money is involved, public accountability must be absolute.

For the private sector developer, grants are also the easiest to administer, although the effect on cash flow of a grant or loan may both be favourable. Although a grant is normally more attractive, in both cash flow terms and as no conditions apply which have not been satisfied at the outset, government loan finance in a project can provide ready access to additional capital funds should the project require assistance, and if government wishes to preserve its original investment.

The choice for government as to whether to give grant aid or loan finance to a specific project, or to a tourism development in general, will be a political decision, influenced by many factors. Loans are politically more widely acceptable, as the perceived direct cost to public funds will only be the *preferential* element of the loan, as opposed to the whole amount of a grant whilst the economic and social benefits will be very similar – for example, employment opportunities, tax revenues, provision of leisure facilities etc.

The financial benefits of loans are also readily quantifiable, for example the number of jobs created, or the amount of tax revenue received: they are politically presentable and acceptable, and easily understood. Grants in kind – the provision of land, the development of essential infrastructure – carry the least risk of all forms of financial aid. State owned land which is developed has a greater value than undeveloped land, and the provision of infrastructure is the creation of social capital which contributes to the wealth of a country, and aids further development.

Quasi-financial incentives – These include loan guarantees, subsidies and exchange rate guarantees where the cash outlay from public funds is reduced, or in some cases nil, but government clearly states its confidence in the project.

Financial incentives in the form of grants and loans are the best method of promoting and directing tourism development, by removing obstacles to project profitability. Paradoxically, those economies with immature tourism sectors which could most benefit from overall growth are often those with insufficient access to funds, and are therefore unable to offer assistance in a planned, comprehensive manner.

Such countries are often perceived by private sector funding sources as risk areas for investment, and therefore regardless of project profitability, private sector developers can experience difficulties in project financing. In these circumstances governments can provide loan guarantees to commercial funding sources, to demonstrate their commitment and confidence in the tourism sector, at an initial cost and, in most cases, no cost at all to public funds.

Alternatively a government may choose to make a financial commitment by offering a loan subsidy or *interest relief grant* which finances the differential between the (commercial) rate of interest charged by the lending institution, and a lower rate decided by the government (which may be fixed, or may be related to the flexible commercial rate). This form of incentive requires no large initial injection of funds, and the outlay is spread over a number of years.

When there is an element of foreign currency loan funding in a project, governments can offer a quasi-financial incentive in the form of an exchange rate guarantee. The exchange rate for loan interest and capital payment is fixed, and the government undertakes to relieve any adverse effects from exchange rate fluctuations. This form of incentive therefore alleviates one form of risk associated with tourism development in areas where exchange rate fluctuations can seriously affect profitability.

Fiscal incentives – These can have the dual role of removing obstacles to project profitability, where this would otherwise be marginal, and of accelerating the development process by making the investment climate more attractive than that in another destination. Fiscal incentives can apply both to the development stage of a project and to the actual operation of the facility. They can be specific to the tourism sector or, more usually, are part of an overall economic policy aimed at encouraging capital investment, and particularly at attracting foreign investment. In general, fiscal incentives preserve or increase profits during operation, although some are intended to reduce the initial construction cost through duty exemption etc.

A particular feature of most fiscal incentives, of both political and economic significance, is that the benefit to the developer often will not accrue until the project is profitable, and therefore is no longer in need of assistance. A careful assessment of projects will identify those developments of marginal profitability for which a fiscal incentive will actually realise a surplus.

Examples of fiscal incentives are:

- Profits tax reductions;
- Net operating loss carry-over;
- Tax credit on interest on foreign loans;
- Real estate tax exemption;
- Preferential energy tariffs;
- Reduced importation duties on equipment;
- Tax credits on domestic capital equipment;
- Tax exemption on re-invested profits;
- Capital expenditure allowances.

Because they generally have no significant effect upon the cash flow in the early years of a tourism project (unless they can be used against profits generated by other activities), fiscal incentives are most commonly used in conjunction with financial incentives. The cost related to the provision of fiscal incentives is readily assessed, as they are specific eg 50 per cent profits tax reduction is easily measured. However, the benefits accruing to government (as opposed to the private sector, whose benefit is equal to the cost of the government) are less readily measured. Where a grant or loan is offered, it is often the case that the project would not have been realised without it – and indeed this may be a condition for obtaining the award. It is therefore appropriate for all the benefits accruing from the project to be directly related to the cost of the incentive. Such ease of measurement is not possible with fiscal incentives, and their cost must often be written off against more general benefits, such as reduced unemployment or increased per capita income, rather than against specific benefits.

Other Incentives

There are other incentives which are not strictly investment incentives as they do not affect the cost, nor directly the profitability of a project or incentives in that they form part of the investment climate, for example, a policy of promotion and marketing by the government to increase tourist volumes to a region or country will increase the potential market for, and thus potential viability of, tourism components located in that region.

Other government incentives may include the following:

Training	A government may provide training facilities and courses to increase the qualified workforce.
Work Permits	The lifting of access restrictions for where there is a shortage of professional skills locally or to have a positive effect on tourism volumes.
Repatriation of Foreign Earnings	The removal of restrictions on the international transfer of operating profits, capital gains and expatriate staff salaries.
Access to Materials	Where government allow materials required for the construction and operation of a tourism project and which are not available locally to be imported.

Of most importance is the economic and political stability of a destination. Although certain incentives can be offered to alleviate the effects of instability, or perceived instability, project profitability, although commercially attractive, may be insufficient to compensate for the risks involved in development. World Bank lending to nations is often conditional upon, or even intended to achieve, political or economic change and hence stability, creating a more secure investment climate.

All countries of the world, from the most undeveloped to the most developed, have on their statute books measures which are, or which can be construed as being tourism investment incentives. The use to which these are put depends upon the existence and application of a tourism policy; upon the maturity of a country's tourism sector; and other, less tangible factors, including political will.

Impact of Financial Incentives on Tourism Development

Introduction

To demonstrate the potential effect of financial investment incentives on a tourism project, we have assumed the development of a 100 bedroom hotel in a suburban location as an example.

Projected operating profits

Year 1 represents the first year of operation of the new hotel, and it has been assumed that by Year 3 the hotel will have established itself in the market place, and that the results for that year are representative of a stabilised trading pattern. It has been further assumed that an annual inflation rate of five per cent applies equally to revenue and costs.

The operating statement for the first three years of operation of the hotel, with the underlying assumptions, is as follows:

	Actual Year Values (5% annual inflation)		
Year	1	2	3
Occupancy (%)	55	60	65
Average Room Rate ($)	50.00	52.50	55.13
	$000's	$000's	$000's
Rooms Revenue (60%)	1,004	1,150	1,308
Total Revenue (100%)	1,673	1,916	2,180
Gross Operating Profit (35%)	586	671	763
Surplus Available for Debt Service (25%)	418	479	545

Capital costs

An average capital cost of $45,000 per room, on a turn-key basis and at opening year values, has been assumed to give a total capital cost of $4.5 million.

Financing Plans

The following assumptions have been made concerning the financing of the project and the conditions of loans. It has been assumed that interest and other charges incurred during the development of the hotel have been 'rolled-up' into the capital costs.

Finance Plans										
	Plan A $000's	%	Plan B $000's	%	Plan C $000's	%	Plan D $000's	%	Plan E $000's	%
Equity	1,800	40	900	20	1,800	40	900	20	1,800	40
Commercial Loan	2,700	60	2,700	60	1,800	40	2,700	60	1,800	40
Grant Aid	–	–	900	20	900	20	–	–	–	–
'Soft' Loan	–	–	–	–	–	–	900	20	900	20
Total	4,500	100	4,500	100	4,500	100	4,500	100	4,500	100

	Commercial Loan	*Soft* Loan
Term (years)	12	12
Interest (%)	12.5	6
Moratorium (years)	2	2

Cash Flow Projections

We have produced cashflow projections for the above finance plans in order to calculate both the pay back period and the internal rate of return of the project.

Investment Appraisal

The table below sets out the pay-back periods and the internal rates of return achieved in each of the financing plans:

	Plan A	Plan B	Plan C	Plan D	Plan E
Pay-back in year	11	9	8	13	9
Internal Rates of Return %	14	21	19	16	15

The measure of pay-back represents the number of years taken before the net income received from a project is equivalent to the total capital outlay. Organisations may guide their investment decision by setting a minimum pay-back period, excluding those projects not meeting this criterion. Whilst this method has a number of shortcomings, such as not taking account of the timing of earnings before the final date of the pay-back period (cash inflows at the beginning of a project being worth more than those at the end), and not considering earnings after the final date of the pay-back period, thus limiting the economic life of the project, it is frequently used as a preliminary screening device before applying another form of investment appraisal. It is also useful to businesses experiencing liquidity problems which will be aided in the short term if projects with short pay-back periods are selected.

To demonstrate the effects of grant and soft loan financing on the project, we have calculated the equity pay-back period on the financing plans.

Plan A uses the standard financing plan of 40 per cent equity and 60 per cent commercial loan, with a pay-back period of 11 years. Grant finance of 20 per cent, which reduces the necessary equity financing, produces a pay-back period in Plan B of nine years; grant finance of 20 per cent which reduces the loan requirement to 40 per cent produces a pay-back period in Plan C of eight years. Where soft loan finance is applied, in Plan D to reduce equity, the pay-back period is extended to 13 years. In Plan E the pay-back period is nine years.

A more sophisticated technique to assess the potential of a project is to calculate the internal rate of return of the investment by discounting the net cashflows generated over the life of the project. The method hinges on the concept that the future value of money is not equal to its present value. It should be noted that the term 'cash flow' is used rather than 'profit' as this refers to the surplus funds available for servicing debt and equity after the deduction of tax and other cash costs before depreciation.

There are three elements to calculating the internal rate of return:

1. Ascertain the life of the investment in years as the duration for which the return on investment will be measured;
2. Forecast the net cash flow for this duration;
3. Determine the rate of discount which will equate net outlays to net inflows when discounted back to the date of commencing the project.

This rate of discount thus represents the internal rate of return over the given life of the investment.

We have derived a range of internal rates of return on the equity invested in the five assumed financing plans. Plan A produces a 14 per cent return. By halving the equity investment through grant aid as in Plan B the return is increased to 21 per cent, showing the significant benefit of grant aid to the investor. Plan C returns 19 per cent on the equity which, when compared with Plan B, illustrates one of the shortcomings of investment appraisal by the internal rate of return technique. It should be noted that the grant aid in Plan C has been diverted to reduce the amount of the commercial loan which maintains the equity investment at £1,800,000. The investor therefore gains a return of 19 per cent of this sum as distinct from 21 per cent on £900,000.

In the case of Plan D, the provision of *soft* loan at the preferential interest rate reduces the internal rate of return to 16 per cent, in direct comparison with Plan B where the investor is in the same equity position. The benefit of grant aid against a 'soft' loan as an incentive is apparent. Plan E yields a 15 per cent return which is just marginally higher than Plan A where there is no incentive aid.

The factors affecting the investment decision of the institution providing the incentive may be further reaching than a pure commercial return, however, government may place a great deal of importance on the amount of foreign currency and that may potentially be generated by the project or employment. A net inflow of hard (foreign) currency to a country through the provision of an incentive may take precedence over the potential return on the investment, particularly in the short term.

References

1 Martin Gerty, Director, Horwath Consulting – speaking at The 2nd Annual Conference on Developing Property for the Hotel and Leisure Industry, March 1989.
2 Trevor Ward, Director, Horwath Consulting, The Hotel Feasibility Study – Principles and Practice, Spring 1989.
3 This section draws widely from "An Examination of Tourism Investment Incentives" by Jonathan Bodlender and Trevor Ward, published in February 1987 by World Tourism Organisation and Horwath & Horwath International.

Index